Customer Value Co-Creation: Powering the Future through Strategic Relationship Management

By Bernard Quancard and the SAMA community

Edited by Nicolas Zimmerman

www.wessexlearning.com

Wessex Press, Inc.
www.wessexlearning.com

Noel Capon, R.C. Kopf Professor of International Marketing, Columbia Business School, founded Wessex Press, Inc. in 2007. Wessex is a small publisher with global reach focusing predominantly on marketing, management, and other higher-education textbooks. Wessex's goal is to provide top-quality learning materials at affordable prices. Publishing under the Wessex Press and AxcessCapon brands, Wessex Press, Inc. offers titles in multiple print and digital formats. Wessex also offers video books.

Library of Congress Cataloging-in-Publication Data

Quancard, Bernard and the SAMA Community

    Customer Value Co-Creation: Powering the Future through Strategic Relationship Management /
       Bernard Quancard and the SAMA Community

    p. cm.

  ISBN   978-0-9990649-5-5 (hardcover)
          978-0-9990649-6-2 (softcover)

    1. Customer Value Co-Creation. I. Title: Powering the future through strategic relationship management.
II. Bernard Quancard and the SAMA Community

Design/Production: Anna Botelho
Editor: Nicolas Zimmerman

Table of Contents

Introduction

This book has one overarching goal: to help you, the reader, create the future with your most strategic customers. As the architect of the strategic account management program at global automation and energy management firm Schneider Electric, and now as president and CEO of the Strategic Account Management Association (SAMA), I can say with absolute conviction that the lion's share of future organic growth (versus growth through mergers and acquisitions) and innovations will be driven by your customers. The days of a company growing simply by making acquisitions is over. Data-driven decisions and innovations will be at the center of the next period of profitable growth.

Our mission at SAMA is to rally support for the idea that, to survive and thrive in today's B2B climate, your company must be obsessively aligned around building mutual value with your most strategic customers. That means that, first and foremost, strategic account management (SAM) must be enshrined as an enterprise-wide initiative seeking the development of strategic, value-based relationships with a limited number of key customers and focused on achieving long-term, sustained, measurable, and mutual business value and business productivity. SAMA research has shown, over and over again, that successful strategic accounts are characterized by exceptional growth, enhanced profitability, increased innovation, and loyal customer-supplier relationships.

As important as it is to understand what SAM is, it is also critical to understand what it is not. SAM is not sales. Sales is about short-term objectives, about pushing products, about volume, and about commodity-based pricing. It is about sales reps focused on their own planning cycle, about maintaining individual relationships at a large number of customers, about executing a sales strategy and meeting quarterly (or even monthly) sales quotas. SAM, on the other hand, is focused on the mid- to long-term and on the customer's business results and business model; it is about joint planning and collaboration with the customer; it is about managing a multifunctional team; and it is about being responsible for the overall customer relationship. It is about being responsible for a range of business outcomes, not just revenues. And it is about managing a business strategy, rather than simply a sales strategy.

Figure 1   Sales vs. SAM

Transactional Sales and SAMs have very different roles

Sales	SAM
Short-term focus	Short-mid-long-term focus
Product-focus	Customer solution focus
Commodity-based pricing	Value-based pricing
Supplier account planning	Joint account planning
Single owner	Multifunctional team
Responsible for individual relationships	Responsible for overall customer relationships
Accountable for revenue	Accountable for range of business outcomes
Implement sales strategy	Implement business strategy with corp. goals

Acquiring the skills, mindset, and organizational capabilities to engage in strategic co-value creation with customers is more important now than it has ever been. And not only that, but we at SAMA believe (and are backed up by a huge volume of research) that it will only grow in importance as the sales universe continues to break apart into two primary segments. On the one hand, transactional sales will be handled exclusively through the web and through channels, and it will become primarily a back office activity. On the other hand, strategic, value-based sales will be orchestrated by the SAM and executed by an ecosystem of stakeholders at the supplier, the customer, and beyond. Strategic account management—especially when paired with internet commodity selling—is, in SAMA's opinion, the only sustainable customer management model moving forward.

Another way of looking at strategic account management, and of identifying where you and your organization are operating with regard to your strategic accounts, is to look at the four stages of customer engagement.

At the first stage, you operate as a simple vendor. You know you're being treated as a vendor when it's clear the customer treats your goods like a commodity, fixating only on price and not on business value. Since the basis of the relationship is serving your customer at the lowest cost, this type of business is going to migrate to the web and channels (if it hasn't already).

During the next evolutionary stage of customer engagement, you have reached the level of preferred supplier, when your path to success is to "delight" your customer operationally—to deliver the commodity at the right time, with the right quality, and with the right support. This is not a stable model, as it still leaves you open to being commoditized and having your customer take its business to a lower-cost provider.

The third rung of the customer engagement ladder is reached when you have become a solutions partner to your customer. Here, you and the customer begin sharing your business plans, and you're engaging in projects that unfold over a period of time and include project management, implementation, service, and support. This is a better place to be, but it's still not a stable, long-term "pricing power" model. You can still eventually become commoditized through an "unbundling" process led by Procurement.

The ultimate stage of customer engagement is reached when you've become a business partner and trusted advisor to your strategic customer. Here, your long-term plans and investments are linked with those of your customer because your products and solutions have a measurable impact on your customer's business outcomes and even business model, making it extremely difficult for your customer to take its business elsewhere. This, readers, is where you want to be. This trajectory also serves as a perfect encapsulation of the mission of this book, which is to equip you with the knowledge, mindset, and tools to transform yourself, the people around you, and even your whole organization in pursuit of progressing your customer relationships from wherever they are now to the pinnacle of strategic account management: trusted advisor status. I want to take you to the Promised Land!

I truly believe that SAM is the one true path to superior organic growth. But to have any chance of doing it right, you have to achieve buy-in from your C-suite. And to obtain that buy-in, you have to be able to connect your strategic accounts program with your company's strategic corporate objectives. If you don't successfully meld the goals and objectives of the SAM program with those of the larger organization, then your strategic accounts program will be constantly fighting to justify its own existence.

So why is SAMA uniquely positioned to offer what we believe to be the definitive how-to manual on successfully building and executing a strategic account management strategy? We've been in existence for more than 50 years, and over that timespan our charter has evolved in step with monumental changes in business and technology. SAMA began as a business club helping companies better serve their customers as entire entities, rather than a collection of geographies or business units. Today, we stand at the leading edge of enabling SAM through technology; harnessing big data; formalizing coaching programs; and institutionalizing the SAM role, the strategic customer-centric organization, and the strategic co-value creation process.

It is a challenging time for B2B. Disruptors abound, procurement organizations have become highly sophisticated, and the proliferation of data has unleashed forces of change, the repercussions of which we're only gradually becoming aware. But make no mistake: These challenges also create enormous opportunities for strategic salespeople and strategic account managers who are able to harness them in the service of nurturing strong relationships and building innovative customer solutions that impact their customers' business results. Fifteen years ago, many firms considered SAM a provincial backwater, the place you sent former top salespeople to pasture for a few years before retirement. Today, many companies consider it a stop on the elevator to the C-suite.

The book you hold in your hands is the fruit of years of benchmarking that SAMA has conducted with its corporate members, whose ranks include many of the companies at the forefront of the SAM (r)evolution and span the fields of energy management, manufacturing, professional and financial services, software services, logistics, healthcare, and more.

The book's first section takes an in-depth look at the 10 most critical enablers of an effective strategic customer management initiative. Without having the right organizational infrastructure in place, the SAM program will falter. The book's second section charts SAMA's value-creation process, which is a structured approach to identifying your customer's chief pain points, building trust and intimacy, creating innovative solutions, executing on promises, and getting paid for your effort. The book's third part illuminates the key traits and competencies a strategic account manager needs in order to drive the strategic co-value creation process. And the book's final section imagines the SAM of tomorrow, especially the impact of digitalization on the role of the SAM, on the value-creation process, and on the entire strategic customer-centric organization.

SAMA is the only truly global community of practice in the art and science of managing customers strategically. The whole community is a contributor to this book, directly or indirectly, and I want to thank all SAMA members, both past and present. I would also like to single out the tremendous contributions of the entire SAMA staff, particularly Elisabeth Cornell, Harvey Dunham, Chris Jensen, and Nicolas Zimmerman. I also wish to recognize all of the book's named contributors: Mark Katz, John Gardner, Francis Gouillart, Steve Andersen, Phil Styrlund, James Robertson, Robert Box, Carrie Welles, James Ford, Dennis Chapman, Pat Gibbons, Jeff Marr, Jerry Alderman, Brian Kiep, and—once more—Elisabeth Cornell. I would also like offer deepest gratitude to Noel Capon for publishing this book. All of these individuals have been truly professional, committed, and generous with their time and wisdom. I lack the right words to thank them sufficiently.

Bernard Quancard
President & CEO
SAMA

Part 1

The Strategic Customer-Centric Organization: SAMA's 10 Organizational Enablers

Having a robust, repeatable process for creating mutual value with strategic customers is akin to having a stable, functioning democracy: All the various players and parts are important, but without the underlying infrastructure to hold things in place—checks and balances, a free press, fair and open elections—it quickly falls out of whack. Such is the case with the strategic customer-centric organization: The organizational backbone—the processes, design features, and systems—can either enhance or inhibit the SAM's job and, therefore, can be the difference between having a successful strategic account management program and having one that fizzles. Thanks to 20 years of benchmarking many of the world's most customer-centric organizations, SAMA has been able to develop an enormous amount of data around what the best SAM programs do to promote an effective and efficient co-value creation process. And it is here that we begin our treatment of co-value creation and the future of strategic business-to-business relationships.

The Strategic Customer-Centric Organization

Key Success Factors

Key Capabilities, Tools & Process Enablers or Successful Strategic/Global Account Management Organizations

| Organization Design and Structure | Engaging the C-Level | Account Selection/ Deselection and Cluster Segmentation | Account Plan Structure and Process Across the Matrixed Organization |

SAM Talent Selection, Development & Coaching

SAM Process

- Customer Co-Discovery and Value "Fit"
- The Strategic Account Business Value Plan
- Co-Create Value
- Mobilize and Align the Multifunctional Team
- Capture Value through Negotiating and Closing
- Execute Value and Deliver to Customer Commitments
- Realize/Expand Value through Overall Relationship

Business Outcomes
- Superior Growth
- Superior Profitability
- Innovative & Scalable Customer Solutions
- Quantifiable Business Results Impacting the Customer (Value Capture)
- Superior Customer Loyalty
- Risk Management
- Environmental Impact/Sustainability

| Global Account and Enterprise Alignment (including Global Teams) | Knowledge Management Systems | Internal KPIs Financials | Customer SRM/Metrics |

The value-creation process, which will be discussed in depth in this book's second section, is a critical business process during which the company engages its most important customers in the discovery of opportunities to create and deliver value for both organizations. In order for this process to be effective, efficient, and repeatable, the company must do all it can to allow and encourage the SAM to orchestrate this value-creation process.

Based on benchmarking SAMA has conducted with dozens of the world's foremost SAM-centric companies, we have concluded that the most critical enabler of successful co-value creation is C-level support. And yet, despite its enormous importance, C-level support can be difficult to define. Its most visible form is executive sponsorship, which is the commitment from each member of the executive suite to be the sponsor of one or a few strategic customers. This means working collaboratively with the SAM and, even more importantly, with his or her counterpart at the customer's C-level to engage in strategic business discussions.

But C-level support extends beyond executive sponsorship and includes setting the right expectations for the strategic account initiative; defining the corporate strategic goals of the initiative; ensuring the right positioning and visibility of the strategic account organization within the enterprise; and making it known that strategic account management is a corporate strategy, rather than just a part of the sales strategy. It is these latter two elements that, to me, constitute the most tangible forms of C-level interest and support of the SAM initiative.

The second most critical organizational enabler of an effective SAM program is selecting and de-selecting the right accounts to include in the strategic accounts portfolio. This is the last place you want to be caught "winging it." To be successful, your account selection process needs to be very well organized, it should rely on input from across the organization, and most importantly, it must be executed with rigorous discipline. Most of SAMA's corporate member companies exhibit annual turnover in their strategic accounts portfolio of between 10 and 15 percent, meaning that the environment, the customers, or the relationships change to the point where there is no other choice than to rotate an account out of the program.

The third most important enabler of SAM excellence is actually the subject of the third section of this book: selecting, developing, and career pathing the right talent. Designing a competency model that reflects your organization's unique philosophy and business environment is indispensable, as is having a defined process for selecting and nurturing the best talent. And finally, you can't underestimate the importance of building a career path for strategic and global account managers (GAMs) in order to attract the most talented candidates.

The fourth and fifth organizational enablers revolve around what the company does (or doesn't do) to create alignment around designing and delivering value to the strategic customer. The two most powerful organizational tools to create alignment are the account plan structure and the various management systems beyond strategic planning, such as compensation systems, Key Performance Indicators (KPIs), rules, and practices that are designed by the organization to create better alignment to whatever the company promises to deliver to the customer.

The remaining enablers of a successful customer-centric organization function to increase the efficiency of the strategic value-creation process with customers. One involves the design and structure of the strategic accounts organization, which includes factors such as governance, management of key processes, proximity of the CEO to the SAM organization, and others. Knowledge management systems boost a SAM program's efficiency by allowing strategic account managers to benefit from—at any time, from any place—the combined wisdom of their organization through access to successful customer business cases. Internal KPIs and financial metrics, by which the organization can both incent the right behaviors and measure the success of the SAM initiative, go a long way to making sure that results from strategic accounts meet expectations and are aligned with corporate strategic goals. And last but not least, to get paid for the value your organization delivers, you have to be able to quantify the value of your offerings in the currency (i.e., metrics) of your customers. Even in this age of increasing awareness of the imperative of customer-centricity, far too many companies still look inward when it's time to quantify value.

Bernard Quancard

Chapter 1

Ensuring C-Level Support and Engagement

As with all critical transformations in business, managing your customers differently and with a much more strategic approach requires unwavering C-level support. The strategic account initiative will not survive if it is not top-down led, and that starts with the CEO and the rest of the C-suite. Not only does the C-level need to endorse the strategic account initiative as a top corporate strategy, but it needs to define and communicate the key corporate goals to which the SAM program is expected to contribute. That's why companies need total coherence between their corporate strategy and the business outcomes that come from managing strategic customers differently. For example, if the corporate focus is on organic growth, then strategic accounts may be assigned a growth target that is double that of the rest of the organization's portfolio. Not only is this coherence a critical component of SAM program success, it also functions as a guarantor of the program's continuing relevance within the wider organization.

There are infinite ways a SAM program's goals can be tied to the wider corporate strategy, but rather than enumerate them, I would like to expand on one of the most explicit and impactful ways the C-suite can support the SAM initiative, namely through executive sponsorship. In a nutshell, successful executive sponsorship is a disciplined process that selects the best executives in the supplier organization and matches them with their peers in the customer organization. For an executive sponsorship program to be successful, it must lay out expectations for the executive sponsor's impact on the strategic customer relationship and establish desired key business outcomes, such as innovation for growth, collaboration for strategic investments, and others. Last but not least, the successful executive sponsorship program will establish a dashboard for the executive sponsor to measure the impact she or he has on the strategic relationship with the customer and to use the dashboard to self-improve.

To understand how an executive sponsorship program can impact relationships with strategic customers, take a look at DHL, the massive global logistics company. DHL's Customer Solutions and Innovation group (CSI) simplifies the customer experience by providing a single customer interface, coordinating across the entire company, and developing innovative, industry-tailored solutions for strategic customers—of which they have 100, representing revenues of nearly $11 billion. As part of the CSI approach, an executive sponsor drawn from senior management is assigned to every strategic account. These executive sponsors are expected to listen to the voice of the customer, advocate on behalf of customers across the company, and achieve meaningful high-level engagement in support of cross-organizational growth. Not only does DHL put a lot of effort and care into selecting the right executive sponsors, but it makes sure executive sponsorship is seen as an important career-enhancing role.

Let me illustrate how DHL's executive sponsorship program works in practice, using the example of a strained relationship with one of the largest technology firms in the world. At the time, DHL was capturing only 3 percent of the customer's share-of-wallet in its industry, and a thorough investigation revealed that the customer wasn't happy with DHL's account management leadership. Responding to this key roadblock in the relationship, DHL appointed a new internal board-level executive sponsor to the account, whose efforts resulted in a total overhaul of the relationship. After taking on the role, he:

- Emphasized his commitment to the relationship, his view of the executive sponsor role as a multiyear commitment, and his seniority within DHL

- Appointed a new SAM

- Personally reached out to internal senior-level product, solution, and business leaders from each BU to secure their commitment to supporting the account management team in developing and growing business with the client

- Fostered regular board-to-board contact, including an annual executive review

- Served as a prime communicator of, and advocate for, the customer strategy

- Made himself available at the client's request to overcome internal barriers and commercial, operational, and personnel obstacles

As a result of this specific executive sponsorship relationship, DHL experienced 50 percent annual compound growth with the client in the three years after implementation. But even more importantly, DHL has grown its business with the customer from one or two business divisions in one geographic region to three business divisions in multiple countries across the globe. This is a tremendous example illustrating very concretely how disciplined, robust, and structured a successful executive sponsorship program should be. But C-level support can take many forms.

When I interviewed Pertti Korhonen in 2016, he was the CEO of Outotec, the leading provider of technology and services to the metals and mining industry. He told me that he considered it an integral part of his job to maintain daily contact with C-level counterparts at Outotec's customers. He also cultivated the mindset in his strategic account managers to consider him a core member of their team. "When he or she says that he or she needs help from me, I have told them that I'm not their boss. I'm their team member," Korhonen told me. "If they say to me, 'Jump!' I jump."

As I mentioned earlier, it's absolutely imperative to align the goals and objectives of the strategic accounts initiative with the corporate objectives and related C-level support. Take the example of a company that has decided to invest heavily in managing a number of strategic customers differently by (among other things) investing more in innovation, in building relationships, and in offering a superior level of service. It goes without saying that, in return for that higher investment, the company is going to expect much higher internal growth, higher gross margin, better customer retention, and other key outcomes. So the C-level's role is to set the expectations and goals of the strategic account management initiative, measure the results, enforce accountability when goals are not met, and communicate to the wider organization that the strategic account initiative is an indispensable element of the corporate strategy.

On a more practical, operational level, when you have customers you're committed to managing differently, the C-suite has to make it clear that these customers are given priority when it comes to quality reaction time on issues, meeting delivery dates, ease of doing business, and offering the same quality of service anywhere in the world. Last but not least, the C-suite has to promote the SAM brand and to make sure that the SAM role is well understood throughout the organization, that the career path is attractive enough to lure the best talent, and to make sure that the management systems are coherent with the strategic corporate initiative represented by the strategic account organization.

Thomas Hürlimann, the former CEO of Zurich Insurance for Global Corporate, breaks down leadership into three categories: management attention (covered above), promotions, and incentives. "Promotion sends very important signals," Hürlimann says. "Every time you promote someone, think about this: 'Is this supporting the way I want to drive the organization, or is this just the status quo?'"

Zurich's success speaks for itself. Over the first 11 years of Zurich's global strategic accounts program, the global accounts portfolio grew to 50 percent of Zurich's total revenues while representing just 7 percent of the company's total customers; the retention rate for strategic customers grew from 90 percent to 95 percent; and Zurich doubled its product density with its strategic accounts, from an average of four products per customer to eight.

When it comes to incentives, there are myriad ways to build a system that rewards customer-centric behavior. In 2013 Hürlimann introduced a global bonus pool, meaning that whether someone is working in Australia or Argentina, he or she is part of the same bonus pool. This way, people are incentivized to work for the benefit of the customer, not their personal fiefdom. Doug Baker, the CEO of Ecolab, makes sure his company's incentive systems are designed to keep the best people working in its strategic accounts organization by offering equity pay for its strategic account teams and spots on the general management team for leaders of the largest strategic accounts.

(Bernard Quancard)

Chapter 2

Selecting the Right Strategic Accounts

Selecting the right strategic accounts is certainly one of the most critical organizational enablers of a successful strategic account management initiative. A good way to introduce the subject is to show statistics from SAMA's biennial "Survey on Current Trends and Practices in Strategic Account Management." As you can see in Figure 2, there are two broad areas of criteria one can use to select and deselect accounts. The first relates to the customer's opportunity (or attractiveness) potential, with quantified measures such as past and current revenue, business growth, potential revenue, customer's market leadership position, and the like. The second relates to what we call "strategic fit." In terms of importance, strategic fit is followed closely by the level of trust and openness in the customer relationship.

Figure 2   Criteria used to select strategic accounts

Importance Ranking		% using for SA selection		
		2009	2011	2013
4	Past/current revenue size	82%	80%	79%
3	Business growth/increased opportunities	78%	71%	68%
5	Potential revenue	75%	79%	66%
1	Strategic fit of the two companies	50%	54%	50%
	Customer's market leadership position	51%	57%	49%
	Potential industry/market growth	42%	49%	43%
	Geographic/global requirements of coverage	47%	45%	42%
	Customer buying behavior/preferences	43%	45%	41%
2	Current level of trust and openness in the customer relationship	43%	44%	40%
	Potential profitability	48%	41%	39%

Source: *"2014 Report on Current Trends & Practices in Strategic Account Management," SAMA*

We all too often confuse large accounts, critical accounts, and strategic accounts. Large and critical accounts are very important for the company because of the impact their size has on the supplier business. However, if these large or critical customers behave transactionally, buying only (or primarily) on price, then they should not be classified as strategic accounts. Rather than a transactional, price-based relationship, strategic customers should be those that demonstrate the potential for evolving into strategic partnerships, where the two organizations share long-term planning and strategy, have linked goals, and have alignment around their strategic priorities. We can give as a simple example a company buying equipment for a new plant. The company can make its purchase based around product and price alone, or it can take into account larger business issues such as overall energy use. Suddenly, the two companies are talking about additional products and services with value-added characteristics that make price a lesser variable in a much larger conversation around business issues.

John F. Gardner—a long-time SAMA Board member and former president for global strategic accounts (and current senior advisor for acquisitions) at Emerson Process Management—looks for customers who demonstrate a willingness to invest in the relationship. He asks potential strategic customers for two days each year from their executive sponsor. "If they're not willing to make that investment," he says, "either they aren't willing to partner or you're a Tier 3 supplier."

Obviously, your most strategic accounts will be those that exhibit the best strategic fit and have the highest potential. Those customers that show a good strategic fit but are small could be treated as strategic customers if their potential growth is high. Notably, a supplier that is in a high potential growth market (e.g., in the aerospace sector) might select smaller customers for its SAM program that have the potential to become quite large, both to balance the portfolio and to add expertise and knowledge to the SAM initiative. A customer like this should only be qualified for the strategic account portfolio if its potential growth is substantial.

On the other hand, those customers that have high potential for growth but low strategic fit are really question marks because, while they may be important to the company, their transactional, price-based mindset is unlikely to reward a larger investment in the relationship. If you're committed to evolving one of these large, price-driven customers into a strategic account, work on changing the customer's perspective by looking to see if there is an innovative value opportunity you can bring them. If this doesn't shift their focus, it means they're probably not ready for a more strategic relationship, and you should shift focus to customers who are more open to having value conversations.

SAMA research data shows that, on average, companies evaluate their strategic accounts annually, which offers the opportunity to make dynamic decisions on resource allocation, coverage, and other critical areas. I would strenuously advise against deselecting strategic accounts after only a year or two in the program. Indeed, most companies will take three years to evaluate whether a strategic account should be retained or not.

Rather than elucidate the detailed criteria around potential and fit, which have to be customized for each company's specific situation, the key messages in this chapter are these: Be very selective in choosing your strategic accounts, and make sure to prioritize strategic fit when making your evaluations. Last but certainly not least, get your company's buy-in on the criteria being used to select your strategic accounts. Critical company stakeholders—such as business unit, country, and regional leaders; other executives; as well as sales, marketing, and strategy leaders—are among the most critical stakeholders who should participate in the meetings to finalize the selection/de-selection criteria. Having their participation will drive improved internal alignment and communication.

Jim Ford, global head of client development at Arcadis, likens strategic account selection to being an "internal venture capitalist," picking the right "funds" from among your customer portfolio. "It's not who's winning now or who's the bright shiny object," he warns. "You have to have a process and stand by it."

Also be sure to take into account that, because SAM is expensive, there has to be a minimum threshold of customer attractiveness—sales dollars, for example—to allow inclusion in the strategic accounts portfolio. Also note that organizational priorities, business climate, and key personnel change, so it is not unusual to see a turnover of 10 to 15 percent per year in the strategic accounts portfolio. With so much turnover, it is all the more critical that the selection/de-selection process be very much shared by the entire organization and that the process be managed in a very disciplined way to avoid investing in customers who don't exhibit sufficient potential or aren't a good strategic fit.

Among the biggest challenges is that salespeople always claim ownership of their customers and can be territorial when they perceive that they are being cut out of the process. Therefore, the strategic customer in-and-out process should include a formal review/agreement process to allow the movement of accounts between the sales organization and the SAM program without too many challenges internally or externally.

Finally, more and more companies cluster strategic accounts around vertical segments. This can be extremely important and profitable because of the sharing of best value practices across a segment. To do this effectively, segments have to be homogenous, identifiable, accessible, and sizable. Global vertical customer segments represent a growing organizational trait of successful SAM programs. *(Bernard Quancard and Chris Jensen)*

Chapter 3

Organizing for Efficient Talent Management

Alongside C-level engagement and account selection/de-selection, talent management stands tall among the critical enablers of a successful strategic account management initiative. Research shows again and again that a superstar SAM delivers drastically more value than an average SAM. It's not even close. So to put it bluntly, talent is war, and the war can only be won if you succeed in having more superstar SAMs than your competitors. And when we're talking about winning the talent management war, we're talking about three things: talent selection, talent development and coaching, and career pathing.

First, let's look at talent selection. "Finding and Selecting the Right Talent for Strategic Accounts," a research study published by SAMA in 2016, offers six key recommendations for those looking to find and select the right talent:

- Raise the level of importance within the company of strategic accounts and with it the integral role of the strategic account manager in effectively managing, growing, and retaining top corporate customers.

- Educate corporate HR and align their support, professionalism, and policies to legitimize, standardize, and publicize the SAM role.

- Categorize job profiles for different types of SAMs and global SAM positions.

- Where it makes sense, add more stakeholders to the recruitment and selection process.

- Formalize internal processes for both sourcing and selecting SAM talent.

- Consider screening *first* for desired personality traits and softer skills believed to be the most difficult to train or teach. Too many companies attempt to teach or train traits and softer skills instead of using them as a filter to select the highest-potential candidates.

Drawing on my more than 10 years' worth of working with SAMA Corporate Members, as well as nearly four decades in business, I'd like to offer up what I see as the key traits and characteristics that make a "super" SAM.

1. **Strategic thinker.** This is the individual's ability to separate the strategic from the tactical; to capture and focus on the customer's main pain points, allowing him or her to draw major insights; to provoke the customer with innovative proposals and value propositions; and to sustain a medium- to long-term perspective.

2. **Accomplishment-driven.** These individuals have a drive for meeting objectives and for achieving results/accomplishments. When a commitment is made to the customer on a key performance result or key customer metric, these individuals are highly driven to do whatever it takes to meet that commitment.

3. **Active listener/client-oriented.** This is the ability to listen and capture the key strategic elements coming from customer strategic analysis or customer business conversations.

4. **Ethical/trustworthy.** This comprises the characteristics of telling the truth, of being transparent, of "walking the talk."

5. **Leadership/inspiring.** This is the ability to communicate and work collaboratively, internally and externally at the customer, and to manage a multifunctional team without having line authority.

Figure 3   The top personal attributes for strategic account managers

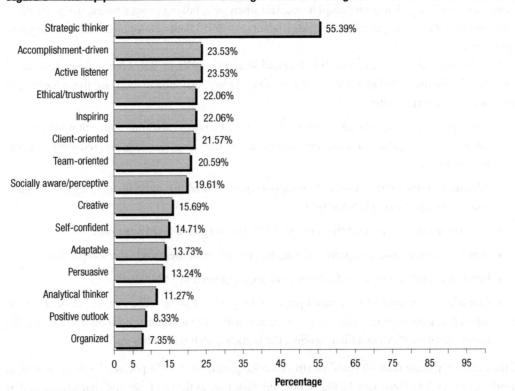

Source: "2016 Finding and Selecting the Right Talent for Strategic Accounts," SAMA

For a more comprehensive treatment of the 10 personal traits most closely associated with strategic account manager excellence, please see "Top 10 Personal Traits of a SAM" on pages 119–121 of this book.

Even though some of these characteristics and traits can be taught, there is a minimum threshold that a good SAM candidate must have in each of these areas to succeed. Today, there are a number of psychometric and other tests that can be used. At the time of this writing, SAMA does not recommend a specific tool but does strongly recommend that companies design the right tools to guide the selection of SAMs with the attributes the company values most.

The second major facet of talent management is SAM development and coaching. While we've already elucidated the key attributes that make a great SAM, let me briefly relate some key descriptors here. First and foremost, a rock star SAM has to be, in the words of The Summit Group's Phil Styrlund, a *great explainer*. She has to understand organizational priorities and then be a *great aligner*, efficiently designing and managing the account and opportunity plan.

The SAM also has to be a *great provoker* and a *great quantifier*, meaning she has to be able to co-create with the customer, negotiate for value, and reach agreement. Next, the SAM has to be a *great connector*, in the sense that formulating, designing, and delivering the value proposition to the customer draws on the SAM's ability to manage and lead a multifunctional team. And last but not least, the SAM has to be a *great optimizer*, meaning she must have the ability to manage the overall customer relationship and overall value journey for the customer, optimizing the business outcomes.

Figure 4   Key leadership competencies of a great SAM

1.	Understanding Organizational Priorities	→	"The Great Explainer" (both at the customer and at home)
2.	Strategic Account & Opportunity Planning	→	"The Great Aligner" (3-year and 1-year account plan and budget)
3.	Joint Solution Development, Co-Creation and Reaching Agreement	→	"The Great Provoker" and "The Great Quantifier"
4.	Multifunctional Account Team Leadership	→	"The Great Connector"
5.	Overall Relationship Outcome Management	→	"The Great Optimizer"

Source: SAMA and The Summit Group

I can't stress enough how critical it is that companies have the tools and management time to coach the SAMs on the job to change the way people work day to day and to transform their overall mindset. To illustrate the mindset, there is nothing better than to repeat, again and again, that they are not managing the customer relationship through their tried-and-true supplier metrics but through the customer's metrics. It's not about "my" own product features and benefits, it's about the impact my value proposition can have on the customer's growth, the customer's profitability, and the quality of outcomes for my customer's customer, whoever that may be. It is not about managing a customer as "a bunch of deals" but managing the long-term customer business value journey.

But on-the-job coaching and training alone won't fill the ranks of your strategic accounts management program with superstar SAMs. SAMA research and benchmarking data always point to the fact that very few companies have a formalized and disciplined process for articulating the career path of SAMs. This is all the more important since, in the eyes of the organization and the customer, the career path of a particular profession or job has the biggest impact on that profession's brand and prestige. The SAM brand will only be as strong as the career path that is (or is not) articulated and implemented for the SAM.

So how do you cultivate the right talent to manage a value-focused customer journey with your strategic accounts?

Rule 1: The best SAMs do not necessarily come from the sales organization. Quite often a senior executive in the following areas—procurement, product management, operations management or R&D management—can have the traits, characteristics, and competencies of a great potential SAM. All these senior executives are, in most cases, P&L holders, which gives them a critical area of experience. The key is to start with the critical traits and characteristics of a great SAM and then ask yourself what roles within the company also demonstrate and reward those traits and characteristics.

Rule 2: When building a talent pool responsible for selecting the best SAMs, which SAMA would strongly advise that companies do, most of those selected should be senior professionals with management experience. Why? Because the SAM job is a senior management job. At SAMA we like to call the SAM the customer CEO. At the other end of the process, companies that are serious about enthroning SAM as an organizational strength need to think about what the career path looks like after someone's SAM tenure is up. Multiple surveys, including SAMA's biennial "Current Trends and Practices in Strategic Account Management," tell us that between three and 10 years is the most common tenure for a SAM.

After that tenure is up, it is essential that the organization makes the next step an executive-level position. After serving as the de facto "customer CEO," it's only natural that the next logical step would be a role as country manager, business unit manager, or a similar executive-level appointment. At Emerson Process Management and Zurich Insurance—two very different companies who nevertheless share a legacy of strong commitment to SAM—many senior managers come out of the ranks of the SAM organizations. (Conversely, if a program is highly evolved, a country manager/business unit manager might transition into a very strategic GAM/SAM role for the organization. Oftentimes, the P&L is actually larger than that of the BU.)

It also must be said that many companies that have a well-developed career track do not force or encourage SAMs to move elsewhere. At Ecolab, the global leader in water, hygiene, and energy technology services, CEO Doug Baker has made it a priority to ensure his corporate accounts program is able to retain its best talent. By offering equity pay and spots on the general management team to managers of its largest strategic accounts, Ecolab makes it possible to have a long, successful career in SAM.

Rule 3: There has to be a developmental pipeline. Too many organizations do not appreciate the size of the leap from sales to SAM. The risk of failure is too high. Programs should consider having a developmental program to identify potential GAMs/SAMs through either a national or regional program that bridges the gap between typical sales channels and SAM. This should be used as a "farm league" to help develop talent. When a spot opens up, you should have numerous capable replacements from which to choose.

To reiterate: Talent acquisition and development is a war, and it is top-shelf talent that is going to guarantee the business results expected from the SAM program. You'll only win this war if you've thoughtfully and lucidly defined the mission and the job, if you burnish the SAM brand within your company, and if you reward your SAMs through well-considered incentive systems and design an attractive career path that will lure the best of the best to the SAM talent pool. *(Bernard Quancard)*

Chapter 4

Deciding on the Optimal Organizational Model

There has been a huge body of work on organizing around customers, and the research is unanimous: Organizational structure follows strategy. In other words, you need to put the customer at the center and organize around them. Indeed, organizing around strategic customers is essential in today's business climate of online purchasing, empowered procurement functions, and supplier reductions.

To be clear: There is no one-size-fits all model for organizing around strategic accounts, because each supplier is different. The key factor to consider is how the customer is organized. Is it global? Is it fully decentralized? Is it a hybrid of global influence but with heavy local decision making? The suppliers also need to consider these key inward-looking questions: Can we scale our solution globally? Can we ensure efficient, global worldwide service support? Should we establish global pricing or country-based pricing to fulfill customer needs and demands? The answers to all these questions will have a huge influence on how a company decides to organize for strategic accounts. Let's look at a few concrete examples of best-in-class companies to see how they decided to organize around their strategic customers.

Figure 5   Market Development Boards at Siemens

Siemens' **guidelines** for KAM and market development:
- **Defines structure for cooperating in MDBs**
- **Gives freedom** to establish unique, market-specific rules of procedure for MDBs

MDBs' **operational tasks** are:
- Deciding the **nomination and cancellation of corporate accounts** and the respective CAMs
- Approving **account business plans**
- Nominating the **project development teams** assigned to major projects
- Approving the quarterly established **MDB scorecard**
- Approving the overall **MDB budget and distribution** key to MDB costs
- Approving **CAMs' targets**
- Fostering **CAM training and coaching**

Source: Siemens

An interesting case study on how to organize to fulfill a corporate strategy for strategic accounts comes from Siemens, the global automation and technology company. Siemens had already started to think in terms of strategic accounts back in the mid-1990s, when it managed some strategic accounts through industry verticals, others through business units, others by geography, and still others through the corporate headquarters. At the time, Siemens recognized the importance of industry verticals, and so it regrouped its customers by sectors such as healthcare, energy, and automotive. For each of those verticals, Siemens set up a governance body, which it called a Market Development

Board (MDB), whose purpose was to endorse the account strategy and decide on key resource allocations for each vertical. All of these MBDs were set up and driven from inside the corporate office.

The next evolutionary step for the Siemens organization came when it recognized the need to separate strategic customers into those that buy only in one geography versus truly global customers, as well as those that buy from just one segment versus those that buy from across the business.

Finally in 2011, Siemens completed its evolution toward a truly global, holistic management of its strategic accounts when it created Siemens One, the guardian of the coherence in tools and methodologies the company uses to ensure the global governance of strategic accounts. It's a centralized, headquarters-based group reporting directly to the CEO and whose main task is to drive the Siemens One spirit and the standardization of SAM best practices throughout the global organization. Siemens One also ensures global-headquartered governance related to approving strategic account plans, approving resource allocations, and so on. This central organization also manages Siemens' comprehensive customer information system, all its data on «people excellence» (i.e., job profiles, skills analysis, and training), and the methods and tools it wants standardized across the SAM organization. (For more on customer information systems, see chapter 7.)

Siemens still has decentralized leadership for managing accounts by division or region for customers who are not really global or who buy just a limited part of the Siemens portfolio. Hence, Siemens developed the idea of segmenting its most important customers into corporate, global, and regional accounts. Corporate accounts are global customers that buy across several BUs of the Siemens corporate portfolio. Global accounts are global customers that buy essentially from one business unit, for example a global automotive customer that buys automotive systems from the Industry & Automation business unit of Siemens. And the final segment consists of regional accounts, which are still strategic accounts, such as a utility or a city, but which operate primarily in one country.

With the organizational blueprint in place, Siemens selected talent with the right blend of experience and attributes to fill each of three roles: regional, global, and corporate account manager. These account managers are expected to connect the whole of the customer organization with the whole of the Siemens organization, driving business-value discussions through in-depth customer knowledge, maximizing account penetration, and guiding a coordinated team of sales, marketing, and technical experts to create value for the customer.

The final component of Siemens' organizational design around strategic accounts is the highly formalized guidelines and operational tasks that are assigned to those market development boards. These tasks include nomination and termination of corporate accounts, approving account business plans, nominating project development teams, establishing customer scorecards, and more. Just as importantly, the market development boards have broad authority to make resource allocation decisions, over and above the BUs and countries, rescuing these critical decisions from the potential mire of siloed thinking. In summary, the Siemens SAM and GAM organization, through its highly conscientious design, has generated significant business results, including substantial growth above market (and above non-SAM/GAM-driven sales), increased market share, increased cross-selling penetration and share of wallet, increased number of one-on-one CxO meetings, and a substantial increase in both customer satisfaction and employee satisfaction.

Software company QAD offers a completely different approach to designing an optimal organizational structure that ensures that all critical QAD resources are aligned to deliver value to its most strategic customers. Whereas Siemens places its emphasis on the global organization and customer governance, QAD places its emphasis on management systems that enable the organization to do what it needs for its customers while remaining nimble and flexible.

QAD's customer base comprises roughly 2,000 companies, of which 75 percent are multinational. Of those 2,000, just 100 customers account for 50 percent of annual revenues, and 350 represent a full 80 percent of annual turnover.

Before the inception of its current SAM program, QAD encountered a number of problems that hampered its ability to align around its customers, costing the company market share and goodwill with even its best customers. In an effort to bring global consistency to its multinational customers, it tested a SAM approach by designing a commission split system to (in theory) encourage cross-silo cooperation under the leadership of a "global account manager." This designation was bestowed upon, not necessarily "earned" by, the reps who happened to be based where QAD's global customers had their headquarters. The result was a culture of distrust, with regions hiding deals from each other, and reps spending more time searching the funnel for hidden deals than they spent actually working with customers. To design management systems that actually harmonized processes and aligned resources around its strategic customers, QAD had to overcome and address four organizational challenges.

Organizational challenge 1: Mission alignment. First and foremost, having everyone across the organization aligned on the SAM program's mission was critical, says Anton Chilton, QAD's chief of global field operations and executive vice president. With the strategic accounts program absorbing 50 of QAD's best customers from the regions and BUs, Chilton knew he needed to offer a clear vision of why and how the SAM program could better service those accounts. The program's stated goals are to (1) defend QAD's position, (2) attain trusted advisor status, and (3) grow the business. "Without that clarity, there would have been much more resistance," Chilton explained. "You have to have specific goals to rally around and behaviors to reach those goals."

Organizational challenge 2: Compensation alignment. All revenues earned from the strategic accounts rolled up into a global team quota, which replaced the incumbent "commission split" system that pitted teams and regions against one another. With everyone's bonuses tied to shared goals, it incentivized cooperation and alignment around customers.

Organizational challenge 3: Executive alignment. To ensure buy-in and support of QAD's executive committee for the strategic accounts mission, the company introduced a common bonus structure for senior executives: 30 percent based on their own team's performance, 40 percent based on the corporate P&L, and 30 percent based on personal MBOs. This structure measures and compensates the team, the total corporate entity, and the individual, thereby ensuring the senior team is incentivized to deliver on strategic customer objectives.

Organizational challenge 4: Services integration and alignment. This is important and difficult to do because, in most companies, especially when you want to seamlessly service a global customer, it's difficult to have the right service resources at the right time and at the right place. QAD was reluctant to build a separate services organization for the strategic accounts program because it would have doubled the amount of "white space" between projects, QAD's biggest drag on profitability. But then how could Chilton and his team ensure the various service organizations behaved in a consistent manner? First, Chilton took responsibility for driving consistent global behaviors. Second, the company put in place an operations vice president and, under him, "engagement managers" whose role is to serve as a single point of contact for customers who are preparing for big project rollouts before passing them back to service managers.

To sum it up, while Siemens puts the emphasis on governance of the strategic accounts organization, QAD puts its emphasis on management systems that enable the organization to deliver for global customers. While these are both terrific examples, in many (if not most) cases, the optimized solution will be a hybrid of these two, where you do organize to manage specific customers strategically, but you also have management systems in place to create alignment around those strategic customers. As they say: There is more than one way to skin a cat. *(Bernard Quancard)*

Chapter 5

Structuring the SAM Process for Optimal Co-Value Creation with the Strategic Customer

SAM is a corporate strategy. In order to be successful, there has to be full alignment between a company's corporate strategic objectives and the business objectives given to the strategic account management initiative. This means that each strategic account and each strategic account manager must be held accountable for specific business outcomes. A list of key business outcomes would include (though not be limited to) superior growth achieved with a customer, superior profitability for both parties, innovative and scalable customer solutions, superior customer loyalty, risk management for both parties (strategic customer and strategic supplier) and, increasingly, greater sustainability and lower environmental impact. All these superior business outcomes can be achieved only through a rigorous co-value creation process, which we at SAMA call the SAM process or strategic value-selling process. We devote the entire second part of this book to best practices and thought leadership on all aspects of the SAM process, but in this chapter we want to show that the strategic value-creation process is an integral part of the organizational DNA and that the strategic account manager is the process leader of the creation of strategic customer value.

The importance of sketching out the SAM process and showing it as an integral part of the organizational enablers is that, like in all business processes, it has to be integrated into the entire organization, and the organization has to enable the most efficient process. If you want your SAM program to succeed, your company must be aligned to support and drive both the SAM and the strategic value-creation process.

I always take the example of manufacturing processes, which have to be enabled and facilitated by organizational devices, such as quality control, preventive maintenance, and the like. In the strategic value-creation process, it's the same thing: The organization has to enable and facilitate this co-value creation process, and this is why we have examined and detailed all the key organizational enablers that facilitate the co-value creation process.

Let's take the example of a large multinational company that manages some 70-plus global strategic accounts and has defined a SAM process. It is obvious that investing in co-value creation with a customer that is essentially transactional and interested only in price is not a good investment. It's actually a wasted investment, hence the importance of selecting the accounts that represent a good strategic fit and that allow co-value creation as exemplified in the SAMA value-creation process.

Another example would be the fact that the profitability of a strategic account cannot be measured if the company has not defined internal KPIs and financial data that allow some measurement of account profitability. Again, it would be difficult to manage the SAM process without this financial system.

Another example from the same company would be the importance of measuring in the medium term, through several years, the growth achieved with strategic accounts and showing, through the management of the SAM process, that growth came out to be double or more the average growth of the company. And to give one final example, a SAM who doesn't possess the ability to be an active listener would not be able to meaningfully manage the first step of the co-value creation process ("customer co-discovery and value fit"). Therefore, having the right institutional capabilities in place to select and develop talent with the necessary mix of skills and attributes is indispensable to creating the conditions for an efficient, successful value-creation process.

For a much more comprehensive treatment of the strategic value-creation process, please refer to Part 2 of this book, where we examine in detail each of the seven specific steps and best practices from the SAMA community. *(Bernard Quancard)*

Figure 6   Organizational enablers by importance

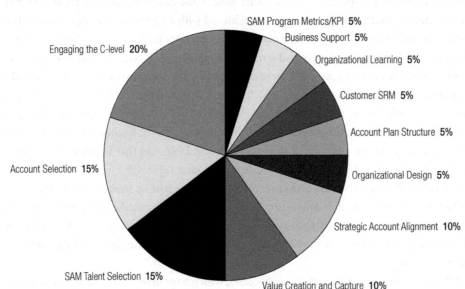

Source: SAMA

Chapter 6

Organizing and Institutionalizing the Account Plan Structure and Process Across the Matrixed Organization

First things first, it's imperative to explain the fundamental difference between an account plan structure as a comprehensive information system for a strategic account versus an account plan as a management tool. There are many experts in the field of SAM who specialize in writing, coaching, and training on how to build a useful, comprehensive, and impactful account plan information system. When we talk about an account plan information system, we refer to a database containing very granular knowledge about the customer—about the customer's industry, pain points and issues, strategic initiatives, key stakeholders and decision makers, prioritized value opportunities, scorecards, and the like. It's a compendium, if you will, of all the data collected during each step of the SAM process, as detailed in this book's second section. This is what people typically refer to as an account plan. It's what a SAM would use to prepare for a presentation with the C-suite or a quarterly business review, for instance.

But when we talk about the account plan as a management tool, it should be short and precise and should include action plans so that the core and extended account team, as well as all the stakeholders involved in the design and delivery of customer value, know exactly what to do and for what they will be held accountable.

Figure 7 Strategic account business value plan dashboard

Pilot Customer – SAMA SAM Process

ASSESSMENTS	TARGETS	INITIATIVES
Co-discovery, value fit, and the strategic value plan	**Prioritize, monetize value, align key stakeholders and decide/close**	**Deliver, track, and expand value**
Assessments are where teams uncover new areas to win with your customers	*Targets are the ideas, opportunities, and customer requests that require prioritization and decisions*	*Initiatives are the projects, programs, and other efforts that, when complete, deliver customer value and open up new opportunities*
Steps 1 + 2	Steps 3 + 4 + 5	Steps 6 + 7

Source: Valkre

Think of it like an executive summary of the strategic account information planning system. The information system is constantly updated, and then the SAM uses the executive summary internally to communicate with the account team and executive management, and to push for internal resources. It's an invaluable tool for internal selling—to align people and resources, to secure executive buy-in, to push for technical expertise, and to hold people accountable.

The account plan as a management tool needs to contain four critical components:

1. **Customer strategy.** How can we summarize the customer's strategy and how, as the supplier organization, can we contribute to that strategy?

2. **Key decision makers map.** Who are the key people with whom we need to have relationships who we need to convince through our value offerings and the monetization of those value offerings?

3. **Past and future value opportunities and the monetization thereof.** How much has the customer spent with us, the supplier, in the past? While it is important to have a record of past value opportunities to show the customer the value we have brought, it is equally important to uncover new value opportunities—which also must be monetized to allow the customer to make informed decisions.

4. **Current and future projects.** How do we itemize current projects and future initiatives, the key stakeholders responsible for executing them, and the means and methods by which to hold those people accountable?

Let me offer a brief, hypothetical example of an account plan as management tool from the world of oil and gas.

Say a large, global multinational oil and gas company has as a key part of its strategy to own its own data processing center to manage an increasing volume of data coming from its customers. After processing all this data, the company hopes to come up with value-based products and services that bring new productivity outcomes to its customers. If in your account plan as a management tool you do not mention this very specific aspect of the customer's strategy, which is unusual because an oil and gas company will typically focus its strategy on extraction and processing, you would be missing a key insight linking your capabilities to the customer's strategy.

The second component of the account plan as a management tool is a laser focus on the key decision makers at the customer, which of course stretches way beyond Procurement and should include not only the chief information officer but also the newly created job of chief digital officer. Again, the key in this account plan as a management tool would be to focus on the management of the critical relationship with the chief digital officer and other key decision makers.

The third part of the account plan as a management tool includes monetization of the value. In this case, the data center supplier could offer software systems that impact the safety, reliability, and processing speed of the data center. The measurement would need to be straightforwardly summarized in the customer's own language and incorporated into the account plan.

Last but not least, an account plan as a management tool needs to detail "who does what when" and measure accountability. In this case, it would look almost like a project management spreadsheet where all the key actions are itemized, the key leaders are matched up with action items, and all the accountability metrics are lined up and reviewed by management.

At Johnson Controls, Inc. (JCI), the global technology conglomerate and a long-time SAMA Corporate Member company, an account plan is treated as mere speculation until it has been validated by the customer at multiple levels, says Mark Katz, JCI's vice president for commercial excellence:

"Do we understand your strategies, challenges, key success factors? Have we properly identified how we can create value? What focused investments will be required to make an impact? How do we measure success?"

JCI believes so strongly in the process of building and executing its strategic account plans that it has paid SAMs, through additional incentives, to build and share their plans with JCI's top customers. It comes from a foundation of belief that a validated plan with the customer will lead to helping the customer win, which will ultimately provide JCI with more growth and loyalty over time.

Katz emphasizes—and SAMA research supports—that companies would be wise to focus less on the template they use for their account plan and more on how they execute on it. At SAMA we see so many companies get lost in the weeds trying to decide how much detail to include in the plan, when they really should be focused on building the best plan and then executing on it. JCI has a simple approach that is scalable for the different go-to-market approaches in its businesses. It follows a format that allows for more detail as a customer ascends the account prioritization matrix, as strategic customers have more invested resources and, hence, require the most robust planning.

Let me wrap up with a couple final thoughts. First, it is critical that companies establish a process of challenging and improving the strategies identified in the account plan. It is absolutely imperative to have a formal collaborative process to test and improve an account plan before presenting anything to the customer. Second, the account plan information system, which often resides in the CRM platform, is an enablement tool for the entire account team to collaborate and stay informed around a specific customer. In a nutshell, the account plan as a management tool is the key for the SAM to execute on the value committed to the customer. *(Bernard Quancard and Mark Katz)*

Chapter 7

Ensuring Account and Enterprise Alignment

SAM is a corporate strategy, and the core of strategic account management is the strategic customer value process. Most of the time, the value packages that a SAM proposes to a customer will involve the contribution of several product, business unit, regional, and country managers from across the enterprise, which is most often organized by product groups, business units (BUs), and geographies. Here we encounter one of the preeminent challenges of making SAM actually work, namely designing and delivering a value proposition that cuts across all silos of product groups, BUs, and geographies. This is what we mean when we talk about internal alignment. (Similar issues can exist at the customer organization, but we'll keep our focus on internal challenges here.)

As a key illustration of this dynamic, please note that when SAMs are asked if it is easier to sell internally or externally, most (if not all) agree that internal selling is the bigger challenge. Usually this is because the company is not well aligned around the objective of co-creating value with its most strategic customers. If you want to get the most benefit from a SAM program, for you and your strategic customers, your company must be aligned to support the strategic account manager and to drive the value-creation process.

SAMA research has shown, time and again, that there are four broad areas that explain the success or failure of a SAM initiative in overcoming the challenges of a siloed, or matrixed, organization. Incredibly, our research shows that as much as 40 percent of a company's internal alignment success (or lack thereof) can be attributed to the skills and competencies of its SAMs and GAMs. IBM, a company that has truly mastered strategic account management, places heavy emphasis on the connection between alignment and leadership, encouraging its strategic account executives to focus their energies on producing innovative customer insights. What does this have to do with overcoming the challenge of working across silos? It's because these innovative customer insights, which create value for the customer, bring more business to both country and product/business units. Even in a highly siloed organization, these entities will recognize the opportunities for standardizing and scaling winning solutions, incentivizing them to involve critical partners in the value chain to strengthen the customer value proposition.

Figure 8 Key factors impacting organizational alignment

Alignment and Leadership: The proper allocation of success factors when dealing with silos	
GAM leadership competencies and skills	40%
Alignment processes	20%
Customer governance	20%
Human resources management	20%

Source: SAMA

The other three critical factors responsible for internal alignment success are alignment processes and tools (20 percent), customer governance (20 percent), and human resource management systems, especially compensation systems (20 percent). We'll start with alignment processes and tools, of which one stands out: the strategic account planning system and its resulting account plan execution.

For an example of successful alignment through processes and tools, we can look again at Johnson Controls, a global technology and industrial company that (among other things) provides products, services, and solutions to optimize energy and operational efficiencies in buildings. With one of its strategic accounts, "Client A," a national industry leader employing 199,000 people across nearly 300 sites, Johnson Controls realized its existing planning system failed to deliver a common vision or strategy to leverage the power of JCI's entire company. The relationship was plagued by poor communication, a perception of poor delivery, inconsistent pricing across sites, and overall poor relationship management. JCI found its solution in designing an effective account planning process, which served as a management tool to allow perfect execution across BUs and countries for this particular global customer.

What was the solution to the poor alignment between JCI and its critically important customer? First, JCI established a SAM as a single point of contact with the customer and the key driver of an integrated account management strategy. It became his responsibility to develop an integrated account management plan to further strengthen the customer relationship, drive account growth, and improve customer satisfaction. The SAM also became responsible for aligning the JCI account team with Client A's account team and for establishing a common vision and goals to meet the customer's business objectives. So how did he tackle the job? *Step 1:* He assembled the team. *Step 2:* He built the account plan. *Step 3:* He organized joint planning sessions with Client A.

As part of this planning session, JCI developed four key focus areas for both organizations: (1) mutual value creation; (2) alignment, namely fit between both companies in terms of goals, values, and culture; (3) relationships, meaning the degree to which both companies' teams are able to work in a trust-based environment; and (4) growth, meaning the increase in overall business value and volume, and results from collaboration, mutual innovation, and joint planning. Beyond the joint planning session, JCI organized a showcase visit to JCI's corporate offices for core personnel from Client A that involved a series of discussions and visioning sessions on leveraging the full power of both organizations for future success. The key objectives of the showcase visit included improving the customer's knowledge of JCI's key offerings; aligning the two companies' goals, values, and culture; defining improvements in JCI's support and relationship management; and improving the current buying process, including but not limited to sprucing up a pricing model that had been inconsistent and *ad hoc.*

The business results were impressive and included improved customer satisfaction, profitable growth, pipeline growth for new opportunities, and improved operations efficiency and standardization. The new account planning system created disciplined alignment and disciplined execution, showcasing to the customer a significant and ongoing level of commitment to joint development processes, leveraging the capabilities of both organizations to achieve remarkable outcomes.

Another incredibly powerful alignment system is customer governance, which allows companies to create a tailored "board of directors" to manage a specific set of strategic customers. Ideally, this board of directors is composed of the main stakeholders within the siloed organization, such as BU or country executives and corporate executives. A very powerful business case comes from the Siemens customer governance organization.

Within the corporate strategic accounts segment, accounts are grouped by industry sectors such as energy, food and beverage, healthcare, automotive, and more. Each vertical has a designated market development board (MDB), and these boards have the following responsibilities and authority:

- Decide the nomination and cancellation of corporate strategic accounts
- Approve the appointment of the corporate strategic account managers
- Approve the strategic account business plan
- Approve the project development teams assigned to major projects
- Approve the quarterly MDB scorecard, budget, and resource allocation
- Approve targets for the corporate strategic account managers and foster their training and coaching

When you look at the overall responsibility wielded by the MDBs, you understand that this is a powerful force for aligning the siloed organization and designing and delivering the customer value proposition.

The final puzzle piece of successful internal alignment is human resource management and compensation systems. For years SAMA has been conducting highly rigorous compensation studies for national, global, and strategic account managers. Time and again, the coherence between metrics and measurement of the NAMs, GAMs, and SAMs and the compensation systems in place have been identified as paramount in ensuring the alignment of the entire account team to customer commitments.

Strategic account management is a medium-term journey, so if the compensation of the SAM is 100 percent short-term focused (i.e., based on quarterly quotas) then we have incoherence between metrics and compensation. Or take the example of a SAM who manages a global customer and has critical team members across the globe. If the team members in different geographies are compensated based on their local results, this is incoherent with the strategy of managing the customer globally. For this reason it is critical that corporate executives and the corporate HR organization design specific compensation systems for strategic account managers that will be coherent, in terms of metrics and measurement, and that will incentivize the behavior and activities they wish to encourage in the SAM and the account team.

To sum it up, management systems, processes, and organizational design that favor alignment—such as strategic account planning, customer governance entities, and thoughtfully conceived compensation systems—are all critical elements for fostering alignment across the enterprise. But the most powerful lever to create the necessary internal alignment needed for strategic accounts remains the leadership abilities of the strategic account manager. *(Bernard Quancard)*

Chapter 8

Implementing Knowledge Management Systems

It is also no secret that the co-creation of mutual value between the strategic supplier and strategic customer can only be the end result of an arduous, disciplined process of customer co-discovery, co-value creation, alignment, value quantification, and execution on commitments. It's a time-consuming, expensive process. So why reinvent the wheel if you don't have to? There is literally no better guide for a SAM in the co-creation of value with a customer than a successful business case executed by one of his or her colleagues.

This is why more and more companies have set up knowledge management systems (KMS) that serve as institutional encyclopedias of successful business cases. When a SAM is confronted with a business challenge with one of his customers, he can simply plug into this virtual library to retrieve the specific case that's closest to the one he is facing. It's like having the entire business knowledge of his organization at his fingertips, anytime and from anywhere in the world. These business cases can even be applied to non-strategic customers, offering a way to scale the efforts, expertise, and value developed within the SAM initiative.

A very impressive example of a well-organized and maintained KMS comes from industrial giant SKF, which has built a multitude of value propositions around their products' total cost of ownership (TCO). This metric draws on many different parameters related to the economics and usage of their products—things such as maintenance cost, product disposal cost, and many more. As of today SKF has in excess of 3,000 business cases of value co-created based on TCO, and every single one of these can be accessed by the SKF salesforce. The critical idea of the TCO approach is to show that even a product that commands a premium price can represent a much better value due to longevity, operational improvements, lower cost of maintenance, and myriad other factors. SKF's searchable database, which includes hard numbers validated by the actual customers themselves, gives the company a substantial competitive advantage versus its rivals, even as its products carry a sizable premium.

A very practical way of using this TCO approach is to create contracts connected to savings achieved in a certain period with the customer. This is simpler than having a performance-based contract but enables the supplier to differentiate itself from its competitors and to elevate the relationship with the customer. This approach has been successfully implemented by SKF with industrial customers, showing clear and tangible results and justifying the investment by keeping it constantly updated.

Knowledge management systems can, of course, go beyond co-created value, extending to topics such as how to engage a difficult customer, how to negotiate for value versus price, or how to use executive sponsorship to get to a higher level in the customer organization. Any of these different areas of SAM practice can and should be the subject of concrete business cases stored in a KMS and made accessible to SAMs and the rest of a company's salesforce. Don't fool yourself: Maintaining a robust KMS is a significant investment, but it's worthwhile because it will become a huge enabler for the SAM and the salesforce when facing a challenging customer situation. It keeps you from having to reinvent the wheel over and over again.

Now here's a question: How do you induce people to use these systems? It requires SAMs to incorporate new behaviors into their timeworn routines, and that can be a difficult hurdle to overcome. I believe the most effective way is through introducing portable electronic devices, like iPads® or similar tablets. Ease of access and ease of use is an important enabler of effective knowledge management system use. Of course it's not just about getting the SAM in the field to tap into the KMS but also getting SAMs and other account team members to regularly feed new business cases into the KMS. It takes time and effort to draft and configure these business cases, so make sure you have a process in place to recognize—or even reward—those who are creating and uploading the best business cases. Also, lean on marketing to do some of the heavy lifting in creating templates and building business cases, though the SAM should always take the lead.

Let's look at an example. In 2015, leadership at IBM responded to a need for greater transparency, immediacy, and responsiveness to clients and the marketplace by taking its global salesforce mobile. That meant outfitting all of the company's 40,000+ client-facing salespeople, in 75 countries, with an iPad, IBM mobile apps, and the sales support to use them. The goal was to give sellers easier, faster access to a wealth of resources, including online social interactions with peers, analytics tools, and market information with specific client insights, helping sellers to co-imagine new solutions, uncovering compelling client value propositions.

The most critical factor in IBM's mobile success is that the company invested heavily in organizational change management. That meant senior management setting the tone that mobile is a top priority, connecting leadership to sellers to drive adoption, recruiting early adopters, and rigorously measuring adoption through analytics. It's too early to have a full accounting of the initiative's success, but the early returns have been promising, to wit:

- Savings of more than 90 minutes per week

- More than 90 percent of IBM sellers using the iPad directly with clients

- One hour increase in sales time per week attributed to using the iPad

Think about how you can create systems, processes, and tools that encourage and incentivize your SAMs both to seed your KMS with proven business success cases and, on the other end, to use the fruit of their colleagues' labor to adapt solutions for their strategic customers. *(Bernard Quancard)*

Chapter 9

Setting Internal KPIs and Financial Metrics and Business Support for the SAM Program

Financial metrics and KPIs are essential tools to use to convince top management that investing in the SAM initiative returns significant financial rewards. Because investing in SAM is so expensive and significant, top management will continue to demand exceptional returns. These returns are measured not only in financial terms but also by predictive indicators, which measure the efficiency with which strategic customers are managed. These are a much better predictor of future financial returns.

Let us talk first about financial KPIs like revenue growth, gross margin, and net profit. These are absolutely indispensable for measuring the financial stoutness of the SAM investment, but keep in mind that they are lagging indicators, since they look backward at what's already happened. Typically, top management will request that revenue growth for strategic accounts be significantly higher—higher than non-strategic accounts but also higher than the market's growth, which would indicate growing market share. SAMA research has shown that the majority of strategic account programs generate growth between 1.5 and 2 times that of the rest of the company.

On the profitability front, and in the medium term, strategic accounts also must generate substantially higher gross margins and profits than the rest of the company. Typically, top management will measure those financial results in the medium term. (There's always the possibility that in the short term, a strategic account, because of consolidated volume for you as the strategic supplier, could produce a dip in profits through a one-time additional discount. But in the medium term, this is typically corrected through additional value brought to the strategic account so that after three to five years the strategic account will generate higher gross margins and profits.) If a strategic account management initiative doesn't generate higher growth and profitability in that timeframe, maybe additional investment isn't warranted.

Just as important, if not more so, are predictive metrics, such as evolution in share of wallet, which is a measure of the revenue that you invoice to the strategic customer as a percentage of the total available market for your offering at that specific customer. An increase in share of wallet will indicate good future revenue growth with this customer. Other critical predictive metrics include customer satisfaction and customer loyalty. There are a number of loyalty metrics that exist in the marketplace; probably the best known is Net Promoter Score, which measures the gap between your supporters and detractors at the customer. Again, the predictive nature of these loyalty metrics is indicative of future growth and profitability.

Still in the domain of predictive metrics, measuring the quality of the relationship at the strategic customer becomes more and more essential. Have you reached the "trusted advisor" status in your relationship, where your perceived value at the customer has reached such a high level that the customer will consult with you for all opportunities, beyond even your present offering and into complementary areas such as logistics, financial risk, and so forth?

Typically we find in the business literature four levels of relationship. First is the pure vendor relationship, which is strictly transactional. Second is the short-list supplier, when you are one of a small number of preferred providers. Third is the solutions partner, when you go beyond just product features and benefits and into offering solutions that impact the customer's metrics. And the final level is trusted advisor, when you share with your customer common strategies and practice joint business planning, almost as if you were one company. Our position is that your company should aspire to achieve trusted advisor status with your strategic customers *while also* being a highly efficient, cost competitive "pure vendor" supplier. Companies that can master this business model will be nearly invincible to any competitive threat. Measuring your relationships along this kind of framework is going to be an important predictive metric for future customer loyalty and therefore future growth and profitability.

Obviously each company has to select the metrics that are the most important for its management to measure and support the strategic account initiative. Once these metrics have been laid out and endorsed, they have to become institutionalized, so it's important that the financial department and C-level endorse the chosen metrics. Most metrics are very specific to the SAM initiative. As an example, if we want to institutionalize a share-of-wallet metric at strategic customers, the marketing department should constantly measure the total available market at each of those strategic customers. Obviously, the Net Promoter Score (or any measure of customer loyalty) has to be institutionalized by someone who is a corporate customer officer and who will use all sorts of measures and information systems to constantly measure and scan the feedback from all customers on all the value offerings and delivery. Another interesting metric used by many leading companies is based on the amount of business obtained in a non-bidding situation at a strategic account. This is one of the best indicators of the quality of a relationship and the recognized value by the customer of your value proposition as articulated by the SAM.

Figure 9   Financial metrics used by Emerson Process Management

Strategic Account Management Measures of Success

Performance Metrics

- Dynamic market participation %
- Account relationship map scorecard
- Customer loyalty index
- Sales growth rate multiple over market
- % of business pre-committed to Emerson without competitive bid
- Progress in achieving "preferred status" for Emerson products
- Quantified business results

Strategic Accounts are a Major Growth Engine

Emerson Process
Strategic Accounts

Emerson Process

2006–2011 Sales CAGR

Source: Emerson Process Management

To see how this works in practice, we turn again to the world-class SAM program at Emerson Process Management and to its longtime president of global strategic accounts, John F. Gardner.

"Developing the strategic account management program and organizational metrics starts with a solid, deep understanding of the overall business management process and the metrics that drive your senior leadership team, both in the long term and in the current part of the business cycle," Gardner says. "There also needs to be clarity on how (and in what ways) strategic account management will help the organization reach its long-term vision."

When Emerson first launched its SAM program, one of the most urgent business challenges was to reduce the impact of the organization's multiple silos, allowing for the development and sale of integrated problem-solving solutions for the customer. Second-order goals included building processes that would open up access to Emerson customers' senior management two to three levels higher than its norm and increasing Emerson's share-of-wallet at national and international oil companies.

In the first session with his senior leadership team, Gardner stressed that SAM represented an incremental investment and that it needed to deliver business results over and above what the BUs and geographic areas could do on their own. To measure those business results, and, hence, to demonstrate the program's viability, Gardner brought together a small, multifunctional team to assemble not only a list of program metrics but also processes to drive each of these metrics. From a starting list of 20, the team whittled it down to 10 critical metrics, which included:

- Customer loyalty index improvement

- Orders growth rate multiple over the core business

- Sales growth rate multiple over the core business

- Relationship map (strength and effectiveness)

- Share-of-wallet in total and for each major BU

- Platform status for each BU and major platforms within each account

- Percentage of pre-negotiated/committed business within each account

- Number of problems solved and resultant quantified business results

Agreeing on metrics is, of course, only the beginning. In addition to program metrics, Gardner and his team set about developing multiple assessment methodologies to benchmark performance and track progress within the SAM program and for each region, account, critical site, and business unit. The leadership team held regular structured reviews of the organization's overall management processes. Every program will have to find the specific measurements that move the needle with its senior leaders based on market conditions, strategic goals, and myriad other factors. For Emerson, those turned out to be growth and share-of-wallet. For strategic account teams, platform status, relationship map, share-of-wallet, and problems solved/quantified business results emerged as the key metrics.

Gardner stresses the importance of providing clarity on metric definitions, why the selected metrics are important, how they're being calculated, the source for all metrics data, and how the data is connected to the business management process. Once his management team put all this in place, the team developed work processes and best practices for driving those metrics and then "deputized" strategic account teams to share their learnings with their colleagues and across regions and business units.

So far we've discussed the selection and institutionalization of metrics and KPIs to measure the effectiveness of a strategic accounts program. But we also need to talk about the dashboard, which is a way to organize those KPIs and measurements in a way that allows top management to monitor the performance of the SAM initiative and to correct, influence, or redirect resources as needed. This is critical to ensuring the continued support of top management. Typically the head of the SAM program will have to train the C-level on the key metrics, how to interpret them, and how to use them to manage and coach all the SAM program's key stakeholders. Additionally, rewards and recognition systems absolutely have to be aligned with the metrics that have been singled out as most important. *(Bernard Quancard and John F. Gardner)*

Chapter 10

Evaluating Supplier Relationship Management Culture, Systems, and Metrics at the Strategic Customer

One of the key parameters leading to the selection by the supplier of a set of strategic customers is what we call strategic fit. An essential part of strategic fit can be summed up in the question "Are we facing a customer purchasing organization that is open to co-value creation, rather than a customer purchasing organization that is essentially making decisions on price and whose essential drive and performance metrics are around the commoditization of suppliers?" Most purchasing organizations that are open to value over price engage in what we call supplier relationship management (SRM), a discipline that mirrors the SAM approach by trying to co-create value with a company's most important suppliers and to manage them much more strategically.

This very different attitude and mindset within the customer purchasing organization leads to the customer looking at many other metrics besides price, suppressing the primacy of price over time. From the customer point of view, there are many ways to improve the bottom line over and above extracting price breaks. At the core of this is value. Value-focused customers will use metrics such as supplier reliability, quality of the supplier's offerings, lifecycle cost of service and maintenance, and degree of innovativeness.

Having a customer who can see beyond price cuts to collaboratively co-create value with its suppliers leads to many of the methodologies and practices common to both SAM and SRM and naturally leads to managing the relationship with an eye toward maximizing the impact the supplier can have on the customer's overall business. When customer organizations start looking beyond price, they begin valuing suppliers on metrics like contribution to growth, cost containment beyond price, innovative solutions that promote the customer's brand, and many others. In other words, a different mindset leads to different methodologies, and that's what it's all about.

And what if you are in the position of trying to guide your strategic customer to a more collaborative approach? SAMA member business cases demonstrate that the best way to change the mindset of a purchaser that is anchored to price is to work on innovative projects. So maybe the best way to teach SRM to your customer is to identify a couple of very innovative project opportunities and use a collaborative approach to work on co-value creation that focuses on producing real business value for both your firm and your customer's. As a matter of fact, in some companies the purchasing organization is sometimes split into two partners: one for existing projects and the other for innovative projects. Once you have accumulated some winning business cases of co-value creation on innovative project opportunities, and the mindset of your purchaser has changed, then you can extend this paradigm to other opportunities and even to the base business—provided you can find innovative ideas that can impact the base business. That's one pathway to change a price-based relationship into one based on value and collaboration. Indeed the ultimate stage of the SAM process is in managing the overall value relationship by which we mean that the goal of the entire value process is to treat the customer journey as a continuous loop, not as a set of discrete deals or projects.

Figure 10   A sample supplier performance review summary

	2012	2013	2014	2015 YTD July	Trend
Quality	●	●	●	●	↗
Logistic	●	●	●	●	↗
Productivity	●	●	●	●	↘
Competitiveness	Not measured	●	●	●	↗
Innovation	Not measured	●	●	●	→
Planet & Society Responsibility	Not measured	●	●	●	→
Responsiveness	Not measured	●	●	●	→
Overall Supplier Performance		●	●	●	↗

Source: Schneider Electric

In my experience you can change the mindset of a purchasing organization, but it's going to take time. It's going to take several projects that impact the bottom line by means other than price reductions, and it takes several customer stakeholders who are willing to advocate for a value mindset. In the interim, there will, of course, be some percentage of business volume that will remain price-based. But the objective of the SAM is to move the needle so that, out of the total flow of business between the supplier and the customer, a growing proportion of that volume will fall in the value bucket.

At Emerson Process Management, the former President for Global Strategic Accounts John F. Gardner draws a very strong distinction between his customers' SRM and purchasing functions. SRM sets the strategic direction of the organization, leads implementation of the SRM's category management process, and, most importantly, is focused on the big picture. Consequently, those working in SRM are measured on how much value they can bring to the organization based on the business's larger strategic goals. Purchasing, meanwhile, is charged with the tactical buying of goods and services based on strategic framework agreements that have been put in place. So critical is the SRM function to the creation of mutual value for Emerson and its customers, says Gardner, that Emerson won't consider a company for its strategic accounts portfolio if it doesn't have an SRM program in place.

Nothing can replace the value of sitting down and having a deep conversation with the customer about its business successes and challenges, Gardner says. "My (and our) greatest successes have come from sitting down with the leadership for the customer's Operations, Maintenance, Engineering, IT, Capital Projects, and Reliability leadership—with the supply chain leader as a partner—to review the current business challenges and where the customer is falling short against the business plan. With the deeper understanding of their business successes and challenges, we're better able to explore opportunities where technology, products, services, integrated solutions, work processes, and subject matter experts can be enablers to solving relevant business problems that will move the needle on customer business metrics."

To illustrate how this works in practice, here is a case example from Gardner's 30-plus years working in strategic accounts with Emerson. While in the beginning stages of setting up a common global operations management plan for the existing and newly acquired facilities of a mid-sized global chemical company, Emerson's team worked with the customer's global vice president for operations, supply chain leadership, and the operations management initiative leader. By brainstorming metrics that would be both relevant and meaningful, the team identified more than 20 metrics that could be used to define the success of the companies' strategic alliance. From this list, they eventually settled on five key metrics:

- Target percentage of prior year sales for quantifiable business results (QBRs) implemented
- Percent of obsolete systems upgraded with the goal of 100 percent over seven years
- Number of opportunities identified for customer products to be potentially used in supplier manufacturing operations
- Joint customer satisfaction survey improvements
- Gains in share-of-wallet for the supplier with the customer

This is a tremendous example of a company sitting down with its strategic partner and developing metrics that benefit **both** companies. This process couldn't have succeeded without strong support from executive sponsors on both sides, as well as the strong relationship, developed over the course of many years, between Emerson's strategic account leader and his customer counterpart. Aligned and committed scorecard metrics are critical to showing the value of a B2B alliance relationship between customer and supplier. Especially in times of personnel or leadership transition, these shared metrics can be critical stabilizing elements. In order to sustain mutually beneficial customer-supplier alliances, **both** organizations must make incremental investments, and the alliance must yield high incremental return on investment for both parties over a business-as-usual approach. *(Bernard Quancard and John F. Gardner)*

Part 2

The Co-Value Creation Process

With the digital tsunami that is invading all business sectors, it is no wonder that strategic customer management, strategic selling, and even sales are hugely impacted. What do we mean when we talk about a digital tsunami? We are talking specifically about leveraging a world of connected devices relaying data in real time, 24 hours a day, seven days a week to improve your customer's business. The focus will continue to move away from capturing data and will coalesce around processing data, analyzing it and offering customers prescriptive advice based on data-based insights.

At SAMA our prediction is that sales will split into two big categories. One will be sales done exclusively on the internet or through channels, and these will be purely transactional—with price being the prime metric at play. The other category will be strategic selling and SAM. The focus of this book is on the latter. This is why it is so critical for SAMA and its community of practice (which includes practitioners, consultants, and academics working in the field of strategic customer relationships) to define what an efficient strategic selling process should look like. That is the goal of this section of the book, in which we will delve into the details of the strategic account management process, which could also be called the strategic value-selling process.

The SAMA SAM Process

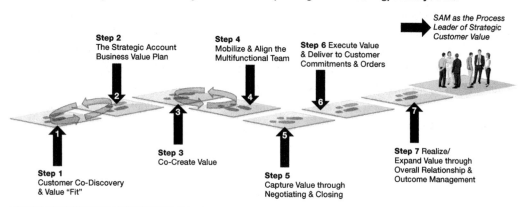

Excellence in the Strategic Account Management Process

Business Outcomes
- Superior Growth
- Superior Profitability
- Innovative & Scalable Customer Solutions
- Superior Customer Loyalty
- Risk Management
- Environmental Impact/Sustainability

Strategic Account Management Process (Strategic Value Selling) Priority Areas

SAM as the Process Leader of Strategic Customer Value

Step 1 Customer Co-Discovery & Value "Fit"

Step 2 The Strategic Account Business Value Plan

Step 3 Co-Create Value

Step 4 Mobilize & Align the Multifunctional Team

Step 5 Capture Value through Negotiating & Closing

Step 6 Execute Value & Deliver to Customer Commitments & Orders

Step 7 Realize/Expand Value through Overall Relationship & Outcome Management

According to McKinsey & Co., 60 to 70 percent of buying decisions are de facto *made before the request for proposal (RFP). There are myriad reasons for this. Sales are becoming more complex, cycles*

are growing longer, the number of stakeholders involved in making decisions is increasing, and offerings are becoming ever more sophisticated. This is why SAMA has defined four critical pre-RFP steps.

The first step is customer co-discovery and value fit, where the outcome is a formalization of the value fit insights and the prioritized value opportunities at the customer. The second step is creating the strategic account plan, which is both an information system and a management tool to formalize all the critical steps of the SAM process.

The third step is actually co-creating value with different stakeholders, both at the customer and inside the supplier organization. The key outcome of this step is the blueprinting of the best value proposition and the monetization thereof. The last part is critical because, more than ever, customers demand that the value you as a strategic supplier bring to the customer be rigorously quantified. Never forget: The only entity that can validate the value you bring is your customer.

The fourth step of the SAM process is closely related to the co-value creation step. It is mobilizing and aligning the multifunctional team to actually co-create the value. The key element of this step is to create not only internal alignment within the supplier organization but also alignment of the key stakeholders at the customer—both decision makers and influencers.

If these four steps are done exceptionally, then no real negotiation needs to take place because all the preparation work and the monetization of the differentiated value proposition have already been done to the satisfaction of the customer. Nevertheless, we know that in real life, especially as we see the purchasing organization becoming stronger and more sophisticated, there is still a final negotiation necessary to close the deal. So step 5, where the SAM captures value through negotiation and closing, is the finalization with the customer of the value proposition and the optimization of the price for the deal. When these five steps have been achieved, it's then time for step 6: executing and delivering the value. Hard as it is to believe, to this day few companies have the right dashboard and metrics in place to objectively document the quality of their delivered value—especially in terms of the customer's own metrics.

The seventh and final step of the SAM process is realizing and expanding value through overall relationship and outcome management. This is a critical step because it demonstrates that strategic account management is not about closing deals but about embarking on a medium- and long-term customer productivity journey. And that's why the business outcome of this step is expanding share of wallet at the customer through overall relationship management. It also loops us back to the first step of the process, where we look to expand our reach within the customer by discovering new value opportunities.

In the pages ahead, we will look in detail at the critical elements of each of these steps through the lens of various thought leaders in each area. There will be some overlap between steps, which shouldn't trouble the reader because, in the end, it's about doing the right things at the right time with the right people, and the SAM process is an excellent guide to achieve this. Each chapter includes a short introduction by myself. (Bernard Quancard)

Chapter 11

SAMA's experience working with member companies and our trove of benchmarking data tell us that strategic account managers spend way too little time on step 1 of the SAM process, which is probably the most critical of all the steps. It's at this stage that you gather all the data and the knowledge on the customer and the customer ecosystem, which will lead to the best value insights and, therefore, the best value opportunities. Few people know their customers strategically. They have basic data on customers, like size, growth, and the organizational chart; but this is not what we call strategic customer knowledge. Strategic customer knowledge is about gaining a deep understanding of the customer's business strategies, its needs, and its pain points in a way that is directly related to its business performance.

This co-discovery of value is certainly one of the most rapidly changing steps of the SAM process in the sense that SAMs are asked to tackle broader and more complex problems than ever. Also, the key stakeholders who either influence or make the final procurement decisions are becoming more numerous, and those networks are becoming more complex. Additionally, with the digitalization of supplier-customer relationships, data and the ability to manage data are becoming key levers to co-create innovative and differentiated value. This is why we have selected as the source for this chapter Experience Co-Creation Partnership (ECCP), one of the foremost experts in co-value creation and the developer of an advanced methodology that takes into account the very rapidly increasing role of data in every business sphere. As you will see in this chapter, the SAM is rapidly becoming a data organizer, a community organizer, and a data storyteller, a value innovator, and a transformation agent. The digitalization of supplier-customer relationships is leading us to an age of real-time problem solving, which is the ultimate objective for the strategic account manager who wishes to orchestrate and drive the continuous customer value-creation journey.

The business case at the center of this chapter perfectly illustrates how the SAM had to become at once a community organizer, a technology broker, a data advocate, a data organizer, and, in the end, a value innovator. The business case looks at how one SAM defined a problem in terms of customer pain and value opportunity, then rapidly transformed himself into a community organizer of the relevant stakeholders and problem solvers, and then morphed again into a technology broker, data advocate, and interaction designer.

In this chapter, ECCP describes its approach and methodology to discovering major customer insights, leading to major value opportunities through the co-creation methodology. (Bernard Quancard)

How One Global Technology Firm Co-Discovers Value Insights and Opportunities with its Customers through its Strategic Account Managers

By Francis Gouillart
President
Experience Co-Creation Partnership

In today's B2B world, strategic account managers increasingly have to be more than "just" super-salespeople. Yes, they still have to hold the line on price, overcome product commoditization, and build multiparty relationships that reach beyond procurement. But these attributes are now just table stakes. High-performing SAMs also have to be the orchestrators of a new collaborative approach linking multiple parties at the supplier and the customer through technology and data that results in new sources of value—an approach we refer to as co-creation. More specifically, co-creative SAMs have to master five new skills in order to become:

- Community organizers
- Dream makers
- Technology brokers and data advocates
- Interaction designers
- Value innovators

In this chapter, we highlight how one highly skilled SAM used this co-creation approach to develop a very successful relationship with his account, the refinery division of a global oil and gas company (O&G Co.).

The subject of this business case is a strategic account manager at a multibillion dollar global technology company ("Tech Co.") whose business is to enable safe, reliable, and efficient operations for the processing plants of its customers. The company develops and sells process control devices and integrated systems that help its customers' plants run safely and efficiently, as well as software that can be used to design or manage operations for the processing plants. The story described in this chapter is representative of the work done by the strategic accounts team, whose portfolio represents about 15 percent of the company's total annual sales.

"Houston, we have a problem."

Our story starts with a routine visit organized by our SAM at one of Tech Co.'s headquarters facilities for a delegation from O&G.

In his role as a SAM, he had been networking inside O&G's refinery team and had learned of the existence of several "Functional Excellence Teams" (FETs) comprising a mix of employees from O&G engineering, process, maintenance, and other functions whose roles were to discover ways to improve operations. Buried deep inside these FETs, our SAM had discovered a person acting as lead for field devices, a particularly relevant job title at a company that designs and manufactures many such field devices.

One of the stops on O&G's tour of Tech Co.'s headquarters facilities was its analytical measurement group. "I didn't even know you had an analytical measurement group," our SAM remembers O&G's field devices guy saying. As a high-performing account manager, our SAM knows how to recognize an opening when he sees one—and so he pounced.

"Do you have a specific analytical problem you're trying to solve?" he remembers asking in response. The answer: "As a matter of fact, we do." It turned out that O&G had been wrestling for years with a problem with one of its hydrofluoric alkylation units.

As a SAM, our subject knew in a heartbeat the visit had been worthwhile. He and his team now had a problem they could work to solve for their customer.

Our SAM had seen his share of alkylation units in his career and knew how fickle they can be. Sitting deep inside refineries, they involve chemical reactors that play a key role in the transformation of crude oil into the various grades of gasoline we buy at the pump. (The higher the gasoline grade produced by the reactor, the more profitable the unit.) But there's a catch: An alkylation unit requires using hydrofluoric or sulfuric acid as a catalyst to "high-grade" the gasoline, and these acids are extremely toxic for humans and highly corrosive for equipment. For the unit operator, the name of the game is to inject as much acid as possible while avoiding "acid runaway," the point at which the acid becomes hard to control and can create a safety and quality problem.

To prevent acid runaway, an operator needs to know what's going on inside the reactor. To do so, he has to don protective gear while taking samples of the process and then send samples to a distant lab, where an analytical expert measures various characteristics of the sample with a chromatograph—from which he deduces whether the mix inside the reactor is still safe and stable.

The traditional method of on-line measurement requires equipment that costs about $1.5 million and needs to be overhauled every two years. It also requires a dedicated maintenance person in addition to the sample collector. O&G's engineering staff had looked at myriad technical solutions to replace the daily physical collection with a safer, cheaper, and more continuous analytical process—all to no avail.

The SAM as community organizer

Technicians at O&G had been working on this problem for years without cracking it, so our SAM knew that building a solution would require bringing together multiple stakeholders on both sides of the customer-supplier line.

Knowing the problem would require significant investment on the technical side, the SAM began seeking executive "air cover." He and his boss, the SAM program head, soon secured the support of the Americas-region president from Tech Co. Having support at the top is key, but it's only part of the equation. Our SAM and his boss also enlisted the support of the portfolio management team, ensuring—they hoped—that their project would find its way into the project prioritization pipeline once it was fully baked. They also knew that, before the account team could even begin tackling O&G's problem, they would have to build a compelling business case to justify the investment of resources. The team argued that if Tech Co. could devise a compelling technical solution to O&G's alkylation problem, then they could bank on sales of several hundred thousand dollars for each alkylation unit like it in the world—offering the promise of as much as $10 million in new revenue for Tech Co.

Figure 11   How the SAM organized the problem-solving community

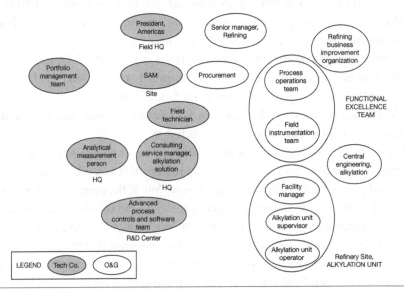

Source: ECCP

Aligning the technical constituencies inside Tech Co. was the next challenge. Our SAM painstakingly enlisted the support of the analytical measurement group that first caught the customer's eye during that first visit. He lined up: the field technician he knew they would need for the work at the refinery with the alkylation unit problem; the manager of the consulting service group that would work with the team on the alkylation problem; the software team; and the advanced process controls team that would, in due time, see how the solution being developed could be transformed from an analytical measurement system into a plant optimization process that would safely push the performance of the unit to new levels. And this A-Team represents just the Tech Co. side of the equation.

On O&G's side, the SAM had to start at the top. Involving senior management at Tech Co. had earned the SAM the right to meet with some of the senior refining executives at the customer. It was a guarded meeting, he recalls. At the time of the meeting, O&G thought of Tech Co. like a transactional supplier and not a partner, with no technical collaboration agreement in place. They did, somewhat encouragingly, agree that if Tech Co. could solve O&G's alkylation problem, it would give Tech Co. credibility as a full-fledged technical partner.

Procurement and engineering had been the traditional port of call for Tech Co.'s salespeople, and they played their price- and service-level negotiation roles with bruising enthusiasm. But our SAM had worked hard at building other connection points in the organization, points of contact he knew would be invaluable in his current pursuit. He had already identified the Refining Business Improvement organization and two of its key FETs: the process operations team and the field instrumentation team. His next step was to see what O&G's central engineering team thought of the project. To his dismay, the team expressed extreme pessimism toward the project based on the history of failed attempts to fix the refining group's alkylation problems. When the SAM asked for permission to visit one of O&G's plants with the alkylation problem, they agreed—grudgingly. Given the tepid endorsement from the refining group's central engineering people, the plant operators were commensurately lukewarm. Their attitude, the SAM recalls, boiled down to "Come back and see us when you have a solution."

It was an inauspicious start to the co-creation process…

The SAM as dream maker

The account manager's breakthrough came from a connection he orchestrated between two extraordinary individuals, one each on the customer and supplier side.

During one of his visits at the targeted refinery, he'd seen firsthand the onerous steps required to fully protect the O&G employee responsible for sampling the troubled alkylation unit. Considering Tech Co.'s stated core mission is to enable safe, reliable and efficient operations for its customers, the SAM couldn't help but think that what he'd witnessed was none of the three. There was, he knew, a potentially huge strategic opportunity to make a difference for Tech Co. at the refiner.

Now this is where our story becomes personal, highlighting as it does the key role a SAM must play in connecting the human passions and expertise of multiple people in the co-creation process. While working on the alkylation problem, the account manager had developed great respect for one of O&G's operators, whom he saw regularly during on-site visits. While not a degreed individual, this operator had developed an intense passion for improving the operations of the alkylation units and had transformed himself into a go-to expert on the hydrofluoric alkylation process. Our SAM had made an early mental note of this key personnel discovery, hoping to eventually pair him with an equally motivated and knowledgeable partner on the Tech Co. solution development side.

Playing detective in his own organization, the account manager found his "man on the inside" in the form of a scientist in Tech Co.'s analytical measurement team. Speaking with him, the SAM discovered that the scientist had developed a theory whereby two separate measurements relevant to the alkylation problem could be combined to generate a third one, which he believed could hold the key to continuously measuring the state of alkylation process inside a reactor—holding the promise of removing all physical human intervention in the process, with its tremendous safety and cost implications. The account manager knew he had the perfect co-creative catalyst in the form of the scientist, who clearly craved a testing ground for his novel hypothesis.

The operator at the customer's alkylation unit and the Tech Co. scientist represented an odd couple in many ways, yet they both played a key role in energizing the broad community of players the SAM orchestrated.

"Without these two people," the Tech Co. SAM says, "we would never have gotten there."

The SAM as technology broker, data advocate, and interaction designer

In the end, the solution to the refinery's problem turned out to be a Tech Co.-proprietary process measurement system (a "platform") that continuously generates data on what goes on inside the reactor. More precisely, it measures the amount of acid, water, and what are known as "acid-soluble oils." It involves an integrated panel-mounted system that is installed in the alkylation unit, which continuously measures the flow and output of the reactor, ensuring that operations are proceeding smoothly. Since it's a direct chemical measurement, no physical human intervention is required.

Now compare the nature of interactions between our various protagonists before and after the advent of Tech Co.'s new platform and the data it generates.

Before: We had a process-based, sequential series of steps whereby the operator would put on protective gear to draw a sample, take the sample to the lab, have the lab analyze the results on the chromatograph, and then communicate the result back to the unit—at which point the reactor team would adjust the amount of acid being used to stay within the desired parameters. Meanwhile, the lab had to maintain protocols for the analysis, as did the maintenance, safety, and health people responsible for the unit.

Now: All these discrete and sequential interactions have collapsed into what can be described as a collective "brain," whereby the refinery operators can make decisions on the fly by simply looking at the system's real-time data stream. Rather than being relegated to the roles of passive data recipients, the lab operators have become active problem-solvers continuously interpreting what they see. They are connected to other resources within the plant (e.g., engineering, maintenance, safety, and health) and can enlist their help as they see fit.

Tech Co. also has access to this new data stream, becoming smarter as more data is collected and bringing to O&G the fruits of this new-found intelligence. Over time, they hope to capture additional data, expanding the scope of problems being solved. Together, the group "co-creates" the best solution at any given time, continuously improving not only the use of the platform but the platform itself.

In the end, our SAM orchestrated a complete rewiring of human interactions inside and outside the alkylation unit thanks to the data platform his hand-picked team created together.

The SAM as value innovator

The final characteristic of a co-creative SAM is the ability to create value for both supplier and customer. The most common form of co-created value is to have the supplier rewarded with more sales in exchange for lowering the customer's operating costs. But as the Tech Co. case illustrates, value can mean risk reduction, lower capital expenses, or revenue increases. As a general rule, co-creation business cases tend to have multiple layers for both supplier and customer.

In the case of Tech Co., the SAM generated value for the refinery in three areas:

- The new system dramatically reduces the risk for the refiner. The Tech Co. solution reduces hazard exposure by reducing the frequency of testing and analysis of results. The new real-time measurement system produces a dramatic improvement in the alkylation unit's risk grade.

- The new platform cuts operational cost by reducing use of the lab chromatograph and the associated manpower and maintenance expenses. It also eliminates the need for the full-time, highly qualified operator who previously handled maintenance on the installation.

- Finally, the solution allows the refiner to increase revenues by producing a higher-grade, more valuable gasoline through the use of what are known as "advanced process controls." Thanks to the data produced by the on-line process control system, the reactor can be pushed closer to its limits without triggering the acid runaway O&G feared when operators had access only to periodic sampling of the liquid inside the reactor.

Meanwhile, Tech Co. has been able to create value for itself in four layers:

- The Tech Co. SAM sold the first unit of the new system at the refinery where the technology was developed, generating a sale of several hundred thousand dollars.

- Its success there allowed Tech Co. to migrate the platform to ten other alkylation units at O&G, generating total sales in excess of $5 million.

- With the locations of all worldwide alkylation units of this type a matter of public record, Tech Co. has been able to sell its new and improved system to other oil and gas companies, including many with whom the company had no previous relationship.

- Impressed by Tech Co.'s ability to develop an innovative process control system for its alkylation problem, O&G also tasked Tech Co. with developing and marketing another process measurement solution O&G developed in house. This will produce yet another revenue layer without requiring the expensive R&D effort that is usually a cost of doing business.

As shown by Tech Co., successful SAMs are able to generate multiple "waves of value" for both their customers and themselves, which allows them to avoid the transaction syndrome where each new sale requires a new effort, thereby generating a high cost of sales.

The challenge ahead

The Tech Co. story illustrates how SAMs likely will have to evolve and how they will need to learn to orchestrate a process of co-discovery and co-creation with their customers. But becoming a co-creative SAM is no simple task, as few SAMs have historically been community organizers, dream makers, technology brokers, data advocates, interaction designers, and value innovators. Every one of these attributes represents a skill that will need to be developed.

The good news is that co-creation is already practiced in some form by most organizations. Salespeople are often instinctive network-builders. They are often quite intuitive about understanding their customers' experiences. They also know that the development of a business case is a sine qua non of business relationships. All of these are great qualities to build on. The challenge for more traditional salespeople is to layer new skills on top of what they already do well.

The other good news is that SAMs will not have to do everything themselves. Our SAM didn't have to personally develop the process-control platform or analyze the data that came out of it. But he did have to orchestrate the development. He didn't have to personally lead all the meetings that took place between the various community members working on the O&G problem, but he did have to bring together the winning coalition of resources and orchestrate the engagement process between them. He didn't have to personally design the entire operating model of how the refinery operators would work in combination with the new platform, but he did have to coach them on how to do it. And finally, he didn't have to close every single sale, but he did have to coordinate and integrate all these sales into a global relationship with O&G.

For most SAMs, a good place to start on the road to co-creation is to pick a customer who exhibits a few desirable characteristics, such as having a good relationship with you, being open to the notion of engaging others inside his or her own organization (particularly executives!), and being open to innovation. The best approach is to do some research and fieldwork, generate a few internal hypotheses on where value could come from for this customer, and then engage the customer by identifying a problem where the creation of a problem-solving community across supplier and customer would make sense. Tell the customer you'll make him or her a hero in their own organization. You may be surprised to discover how receptive he or she will be to this open-ended co-creation approach.

Chapter 12

In the previous chapter, we covered step 1 of the SAM process, which is customer co-discovery and value fit. We emphasized that one of the key outputs of that step is a set of insights and prioritized opportunities. The strategic account business value plan, step 2, is both an information system and a management tool to formalize all the critical steps of the SAM process. The latter steps of the SAM process (to be covered in chapters 13-17) include co-creation of value, mobilizing and aligning the multifunctional team, capturing value through negotiation and closing, executing value, and realizing and expanding value through overall relationship and outcome management. All these steps need to be formalized in the account plan information system, and that's what will be detailed in this chapter. Just as importantly, the account plan is used as a management tool to monetize co-created value, to get customer recognition and validation of the monetized value, and to formalize who from the multifunctional team is going to be mobilized to co-create and deliver the value.

Typically an account plan as a management tool will include an appendix, which will detail all the critical action plans, key players, who is accountable for what, and key milestones and target dates needed to create and deliver the value. This tool is also used by management on business reviews and progress reports with the strategic customer in the course of the value journey. One of the big differentiators of effective and efficient SAM organizations is the degree of formalization and discipline in executing on the value to be designed and delivered to the customer. So from that point of view, the account plan is an essential management tool to ensure alignment of critical resources and accountability of customer outcomes.

This next chapter, written by Steve Andersen of Performance Methods, Inc. (PMI), a renowned expert in strategic account business planning, will cover all the major points we just touched on and delve into the steps necessary to design and implement an effective strategic account planning system. (Bernard Quancard)

Transforming the Customer Experience:

Planning to Grow with your Most Important Accounts

By Steve Andersen
President and Founder
Performance Methods, Inc.

Account planning and management, whether you prefer the strategic, key, or global flavor (SAM/KAM/GAM, hereafter referred to only as "SAM") is as hot a topic today as it has ever been. Why? Because within most industries, there is a "race" of sorts to see who can become most relevant to their most important customers, a race which is certain to have many more losers than winners. In this chapter, I will outline the 10 factors most responsible for effective strategic account planning.

1: Define what constitutes a strategic account and assess ongoing performance

Our client work has taught us much about the importance of defining strategic or key accounts and communicating this effectively, both internally and with your selected customers. Experience shows that the account selection process is typically ongoing and a critical component of any successful SAM program. While at first glance the accounts and customer relationships that are most important to your business may seem to be obvious, on closer inspection it is usually the case that these decisions can be challenging and even stressful to an organization.

How can something that sounds so good for both you and your customer become such a difficult decision process? Among other factors, it depends in part on the customer's willingness to partner with you, as most providers have limited resources and wish to focus on a select number of key customer relationships and to deploy resources accordingly. Additionally, we have observed companies make significant investments in customer relationships they once considered strategic only to see them devolve into futile expenditures due to the customers' unwillingness to enter into relationships in which all parties could benefit.

The last word of this "success factor" is performance, and we're not just talking about your own. Why? Because unless you are conducting an ongoing assessment of just how effective your so-called strategic customer relationship is, you can find yourself investing significant time, resources, attention, and organizational focus on a customer that is more willing to receive the benefits of strategic customer status than they are to engage in an authentic, symbiotic partnership that is mutually beneficial to you both. When this happens, deselection is just around the corner, which is never an easy thing for either the provider or the customer. Also consider the other customer that could have been the focus of the account planning and management energy that was invested in the deselected account; it's hard not to think about the opportunity cost of investing time and resources in the wrong customer relationship.

2: Discover what your customer values most and validate it

Let's be clear: What we're not talking about here is value articulation, value co-creation, or value realization. We're not there yet. But what we are about to unpack is the importance of doing the co-discovery required before any of these other value-focused activities can take place. And it's called co-discovery because you can't do it by yourself. Unless your customer is engaged in this process with you, it's not likely to happen, and even if it does (at one level or another), you can't be sure you've got it right until the guest of honor, your customer, takes its seat at the value co-discovery table.

When you study and immerse yourself in something long enough, it's expected that the picture will become clear, and what was once vague and murky will become easier to understand and analyze. Yet this important component of successful account planning is missed by even some of the most experienced account managers, and our experience is that even the "best of the best" have to be reminded of the significance of value co-discovery. Its significance goes far beyond the insights that the account manager may glean from his or her conversations with the customer about the things that matter most to them, and this is because simply facilitating an effective "value conversation" with the customer can be a significant differentiator when engaging effectively with strategic accounts.

Effective value co-discovery requires that you and your customer explore the things they value most and, in the process, identify potential value targets for future consideration. Think of this as a visioning exercise with your customer, one in which there is no downside—only upside. Why?

Because if you are the only one of your customer's providers that is engaging in these types of discussions, you are almost certain to hear about things that your competitors are not and will be very likely to get that "first whiff" of new opportunities out on the horizon. But keep this in mind: Before ending a co-discovery value conversation with your customer, make sure that you ask why this matters to them personally and, when you do, be prepared to receive something truly precious: Your customer may be about to tell you what success looks like to him or her, and you need to consider this an invitation to help achieve it.

3: Assess and strengthen your most strategic relationships with the customer

At this moment, it is likely that there is someone posting something on a blog or social media about the obsolescence of customer relationships in the modern era of business. Some actually seem to believe that, in B2B commerce, today's customers don't care about developing trust-based relationships with their most important suppliers—and that even if they did, no one has time or patience for this anymore. But fear not, because these writers, bloggers, and misinformed pundits are the people with whom the effective account manager should love to compete.

Contrary to what these prognosticators may think, the development of strong relationships is a main component of any successful SAM program. You'll never see an effective SAM program or successful strategic account manager who is not committed to developing trust-based customer relationships with their most important customers. But what seems less obvious to many organizations is the importance of conducting ongoing assessment and measurement of these relationships. Think of it this way: If you don't understand the true nature of the relationship through the eyes of the customer, how can you build a logical plan to grow and expand this relationship over time?

When we're able to assess the relationship through the customer's eyes, we find ourselves with an opportunity to expand and grow it through the co-discovery, co-creation, and realization of customer value. It's really not that complicated: Customers just want to be successful, and if you want to strengthen your relationships with them and become more strategic to their business, focus on determining how you can help them be successful. When this happens, relationships evolve into partnerships, and doubt evolves into trust.

4: Position and differentiate your unique value with the customer's team

Let's face it: Most organizations feel that they provide significantly more value to their customers than their customers give them credit for. If you concur, then it's important to understand why this is happening and what can be done about it. If the customer truly doesn't "get it" when it comes to your value co-creation and realization, then whose fault is it: yours or theirs? We all know the answer to this question, and top-performing SAMs are taking action. They are engaging differently with their customers, ensuring that the value conversations they began earlier are evolving into the articulation of unique, differentiable value for the customer.

You know you're in trouble when the drumbeat coming from your customer's procurement/sourcing team is getting louder and louder with messages that sound like "You're all the same," "There is nothing different about you or your offerings," "We can make any of our options work," and even "If we're so strategic to you and your company, then sell us your products at the lowest price ever offered to anyone." Is this type of mindset becoming commonplace in today's business environment? Certainly, and the crescendo has gotten louder since the 2008 financial crisis. This is why ongoing positioning (i.e., capturing customer mindshare) and differentiation (i.e., capturing customer preference) with strategic customers is so important today.

The only way to ensure that your value is acknowledged and appreciated by your customer is to be mindful of a few things. First, have you and your organization created and co-created value in the past with the customer? And if so, does your customer understand and recognize this? If so, you can enjoy a bit of momentum by gaining agreement from your customer—especially those sponsors and supporters in the customer organization that you have helped to realize success—that what you have delivered has mattered. Next, have you and your organization developed and customized a broad and deep customer-specific value message that goes far beyond product and solution, including such dimensions as resources, expertise, service levels, experience in the customer's industry, and even your brand and reputation with the customer? Finally, is the account team clear on what the customer is trying to do and why it needs help, and is the customer's team clear on how you and your organization can help solve its challenges and achieve its objectives? If so, great news! You're well on the way to positioning and differentiating the uniqueness of your value with the customer.

5: Harmonize and balance your short- and long-term goals for the account

Based on our experience, there is perhaps no other single factor that has been more responsible for the tension associated with account management than the difficulty that arises when trying to balance the pressures that result from "making the number" in the short term while "delighting the customer" over the long haul. One of my all-time favorite quotes from an account manager reads as follows: "I do my best selling when my customer isn't buying!" When we're working with large, strategic, and complex customer relationships, it can seem that there is a never-ending list of follow-up items for the customer that can (and will) absorb all of the account manager's time. It's true: SAMs can achieve effective positioning and differentiation when the customer is not in buying mode. But it's also certainly the case that exceeding short-term revenue targets is and will continue to be a critical determinant of success for the vast majority of SAMs.

The stress of balancing the short- and long-term objectives that define SAM programs can at times feel overwhelming. This is especially true when priorities are fuzzy and there is a lack of definition and harmony around the opportunity- and account-planning processes. While it may seem obvious that these disciplines should be connected, our experience has proven that in many cases they are not. When this happens, the result can be undue amounts of stress on the SAM, the account team, the organization, and even the customer.

In any economy, it can be very tempting to let the large opportunity or "big deal" command disproportionate attention and resources and take precedence over almost everything else. It's normal and natural to see organizational excitement and enthusiasm develop for pending sales, and when harmonized with the long-term well-being of the customer, this can certainly be a very good thing. When the account manager can effectively deliver the organization to the customer so that value is co-created and realized and expectations exceeded, he or she is, in effect, "planning to grow" with the customer. The account planning process thrives in environments in which there is strong organizational awareness of the need to balance short- and long-term priorities, and when our plans to win harmonize with our plans to grow, account growth can accelerate.

6: Align and connect your business objectives with the customer's objectives

It sounds so easy, and yet alignment and connecting your objectives with your customer's can be among the most elusive goals of effective account planning. After all, if you've done your co-discovery and understand what your customer values most, and if you've developed trust-based sponsor and supporter relationships throughout the account, then why not just "connect the dots" and make everybody happy?

There are many essential facets of effective account management, but aligning objectives with your customer's is one of the most accurate predictors of long-range account planning success. This is because if we can't agree on the big picture (and how to get there), then there's a real risk that account planning will devolve into glorified opportunity planning. In other words, in the absence of an overarching strategic plan to grow that has been forged through transparent and diligent collaboration between provider and customer, account planning can become a glorified exercise in pursuing sequential opportunities that are not necessarily driven through an account growth strategy.

"What's so bad about this?" some would say. Our experience is that so long as opportunities are plentiful and the win rate remains high, the customer and supplier will celebrate each and every win and not look critically at the process. But what about when the opportunities begin to dry up and the customer gets cozy with a supplier who's aligned more effectively with the customer's longer-term plans and objectives? The best time to align objectives with a strategic customer is when you have the wind of "past proven value" at your back and the realization of value co-creation in the present. If that time is now for you and your customer, then you're in an ideal environment to drive the collaboration that will enable the alignment and connection of objectives that can lead to a successful partnership.

7: Develop and implement a proactive strategy to grow and expand the account

We've reviewed hundreds of client account plans in the past, and it never ceases to amaze me just how few include a strategy to proactively grow the account. There's plenty of focus on data, and there's always something about the opportunities or initiatives that are being pursued in the present. But when you look for that strategic roadmap that explains the SAM's vision for growing the account and how and where he or she is going to realize that growth over the long term, in most cases it's simply not there. If it's not there, the only reasonable assumption is that it doesn't exist. And if that's the case, then we've got some work to do.

The essence of account growth strategy is the confluence of past proven value, future visioning with the customer, the relationship between the parties, and the belief by the customer that the SAM and her organization can be trusted to deliver again because they have done so before. Note that when we examine account growth strategy through the lens of our relationships with customer team members, we can look at growth at a more individual level, customer by customer. With this in mind, the conversations that ensue with the customer about what its future plans and objectives are likely to include, as well as what future success will look like at an individual level, can provide something much more valuable than "just" insights. From these types of discussions we can develop the actionable awareness required to actually do something with the information and insights that we've discovered, and this benefits everyone.

An account growth strategy is not simply a summary of existing opportunities but rather a look into the future, based on actual customer business objectives and an understanding of the customer's vision for future success. The responsibilities of the contemporary SAM should include developing a demonstrable understanding of the customer's business as well as the planning and execution of the strategies and activities that will enable the customer to meet its objectives and realize success. An effective account growth strategy should serve as the account manager's springboard to tomorrow's success, and if your account plan is in need of this type of proactive approach to the future, there's no time like the present to begin to build it.

8: Engage your customer in the strategic account planning process with you

Who wouldn't agree that getting the customer engaged in the account planning process can be instrumental in ensuring that we execute on our plans to co-create mutual value that will translate into customer success? Yet based on the infrequency with which this happens today, we can assume that many SAMs simply don't know how to get customers engaged in the account planning process.

Based on our experience in strategic account planning, there are few things more powerful than when the customer takes a seat at the planning table and engages collaboratively with the account team to build an account plan that matters to everyone. However, the element of timing is important when account managers set out to gain customer input, feedback, and commitments that are focused on the mutual planning process. In other words, there are times when this level of engagement between the parties may not be met with as much enthusiasm as others, such as when there is a "burning platform" issue that must be resolved or when you're about to receive that next RFP from your customer's procurement/sourcing team.

There are also types of relationships in which it becomes more difficult and less realistic to engage your customer in the account planning process, including when your relationship is languishing at vendor level and there simply isn't enough trust in the room to provide a basis for deep collaboration and information sharing. On the other hand, if you're viewed as a partner by your customer, it's likely that you're engaging in some sort of collaborative account planning together, and if you've evolved the relationship to trusted advisor status, it's almost assured that the parties are collaboratively planning together.

Wherever you are in your relationship with your customer, there's one very important thing to keep in mind. Customers typically engage in collaborative planning only with their top one or two providers in any given market, which means that the lion's share of mindshare, preference, and trust will accrue to those who are at the planning table with the customer. The time to begin to ask for customer input into your account planning process is now, and it can begin by simply asking for input as you update your account plan to ensure that it connects with what is most pressing going forward. Not many customers will want to pass up the opportunity to encourage you to focus on them and their success, at least not if they consider you and your organization to be as strategic to their business as you feel they are to yours.

9: Implement SAM performance metrics to measure and track execution and impact

Walk the streets of any major city and ask business people you pass if their companies have a successful sales organization, and practically all will say yes. If you ask them how long the sales organization has been in existence, many will say it has been around since the company's founding. But now repeat this exercise, only asking the passersby if their company has a successful SAM organization. The responses will be dramatically different, ranging from a simple "no" to timeframes such as three, five, or—at the outside—10 to 12 years. Why is this the case, when many of us that worked in the previous millennium had strategic account management experiences? The answer may be disturbing, but it offers an opportunity for organizations that are serious about SAM today.

The reason that there are so few tenured SAM programs and organizations today is because many companies that tried in the past to be successful at planning to grow with their most important customers failed to sustain their efforts. When this happens, as mentioned before, there is usually an element of tension or stress between short-term focus on the numbers and longer-term focus on customer relationships. But we've learned some interesting things about effective account planning and management programs over the past two decades, not the least of which is the importance of developing and deploying a scorecard of metrics that measures and tracks the performance of both parties in the strategic relationship.

It goes without saying that today's large, strategic, and complex customers are going to measure and scrutinize the performance of their suppliers, particularly those who represent higher levels of spend and commitment. Despite the pressure that this might present, it also creates an opportunity for the SAM who is willing to engage the customer in discussions about mutually beneficial metrics, including those with outcomes that are just as likely to have been driven by the customer's performance as the supplier's.

Our experience in collaborative discussions between customers and suppliers to determine SAM performance pressure points and hot spots has been very positive, with both the selling and buying organizations showing an understanding of the importance of the business outcomes of their counterparts. After all, why wouldn't they feel this way if each sees the other as strategic to its business and to its future success?

10: Ensure adequate levels of coaching and sponsorship for you and your team

When you consider the numerous facets of managing and growing strategic customer relationships, it is apparent that, on any given day within any given account, there can be many things happening at once. Compound this complexity with the ever-increasing speed of business, the ever-decreasing patience of the customer, and the ongoing difficulty aligning and deploying cross-functional team members, and you have the perfect storm for stress, pressure, internal politics, and even finger-pointing.

Some SAMs take matters into their own hands and engage with trusted colleagues in what might be described as "safe-harbor" peer-to-peer coaching environments, in which each helps the other, and their conversations remain between them. Why do some feel compelled to do this? Because they either don't feel that they can get the coaching they need in a timely manner from their managers, or they feel that their managers grew up in hunting-type sales environments and, hence, the coaching they are likely to receive will be more about driving short-term sales than driving relationship management excellence.

Coaching and sponsorship are critical components of today's successful SAM programs, and both roles require definition and even a bit of advance training to ensure consistency. SAM coaching is not the same as sales coaching, and the coaching and sponsorship dimensions of the modern SAM program are key determinants of the predictability, repeatability, measurability, and sustainability of SAM success. Important early steps in equipping SAM managers to be effective SAM coaches include focused discovery and greater understanding in these areas:

- Why are top-performing SAMs successful?

- What do they do in daily execution that causes their success?

- How do they deploy best practices to co-create customer value and grow customer relationships?

- Where are there performance gaps in SAM execution (even with these top performers)?

Armed with the answers, effective SAM coaches and sponsors can add value to their SAMs through an approach that is more meaningful to the recipient and more focused on driving the right business outcomes.

Conclusions

Wherever your implementation of account planning and management stands on the maturity scale, consider taking a pause to assess your performance within each of the areas of best practice discussed here. Next, determine which of the SAM success factors unpacked herein can have the greatest impact on your SAM effectiveness, and resolve to focus there. Finally, select a few of your strategic, key, or global accounts and ask their perspectives on how effective you and your organization are in your pursuit of SAM excellence.

Chapter 13

We now address the third step of the SAM process, which is the co-creation of value, probably the area that has the biggest impact on the job and the role of the strategic account manager. It is at this stage that we want to validate the value and strategic fit between the customer needs and pains and what we as a supplier can provide. We want to make sure that, as much as possible, our solutions always bring some innovative components so that we are better differentiated vis-à-vis the competition. But most importantly—and this is very difficult to do—we want to finalize and monetize the value proposition, which will lead us to better define the strategy to engage the customer.

So this step is extremely critical because, from it, we will monetize the value created and convince the strategic customer that our solution is unique and brings more money to the customer than any other competitive solution. The Summit Group methodology of Third Box Thinking™ is an excellent approach to co-value creation and monetization. (Bernard Quancard)

Creating Joint Solutions
with Strategic Customers

Phil Styrlund, CEO & Owner
and
James Robertson, President
The Summit Group

Persistent, disruptive forces impacting profitable growth are intensifying, and as a result, companies in many industries face slower growth and accelerating commoditization of product and service margins.

Given marketplace complexity and dynamic shifts in how customers buy, traditional business models are threatened, and new strategies and capabilities for driving growth must be more intentionally developed.

In this chapter, we will outline a pragmatic yet powerful framework for co-creating solutions with strategic customers—drawing on research, emerging practice, and learnings from what leading companies are doing differently to collaboratively create value and accelerate growth with customers in their hyper-competitive business environments.

Traditional sources of growth, such as internal research and development of products and services, pricing, and branding—the capabilities within the firm's direct control, in other words—remain important, but they are no longer sufficient to sustain growth.

Increasingly, leading firms are engaging *with* customers and partners along their value chain to co-create new sources of value by deepening insights, aligning goals, developing joint solutions, leveraging mutual capabilities, and executing together (Figure 12).

Figure 12   Sources of growth, both traditional/internal and new/external

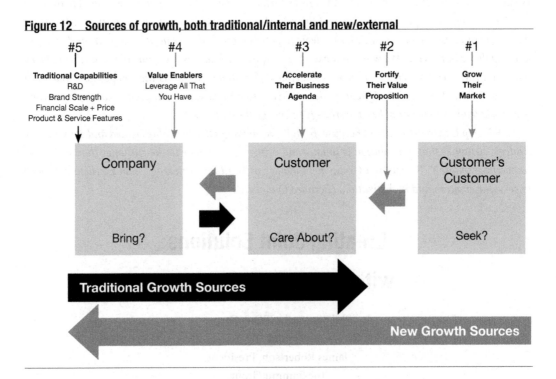

Successful joint solution creation requires an iterative, non-prescriptive, collaborative operating system by integrating a framework, principles and tools, and distinguishing competencies that enable business alignment, customer-driven insights, collaborative relationship development, and co-creation.

Companies should not underestimate the barriers to successfully developing joint solutions with customers. The legacy products, competencies, organizational structure, mindset, and culture that enabled success in the past are likely to get in the way of collaboratively creating joint solutions and rethinking how value is created with customers. Creating joint solutions is a team sport. For many organizations, the level of collaboration and trust required—both with strategic customers as well as internally across the enterprise—is highly challenging. Yet the rewards for developing this capability can be substantial, with leading companies reporting growth at up to three times the market rate and double the progression of their business with other customers.[1] The easy growth is over.

As marketplace change accelerates, complexity increases, commoditization intensifies, and technology disrupts previously successful business models, companies seek new strategies to invigorate and sustain profitable growth—to survive and thrive in this "new normal" environment. Considering the seismic shifts that continue to impact how companies go to market and grow, creating joint

1   TSG/SAM "Co-Innovation Benchmark Assessments, 2010-2015"

solutions with customers has emerged as arguably the most compelling and powerful strategy for companies to accelerate and sustain profitable growth.

Beyond accelerating and sustaining growth, creating joint solutions enables companies to:

- Use the customer to guide, shape, and **accelerate company change and transformation.** Possibly the "grandest why" is to leverage the customer as the central source of navigation for your company's strategy and culture shift from "inside-out" to customer-driven.

- **Distinguish how they engage** with customers, creating value through the co-creation process, not only by what they sell. Done right, co-creation is a differentiating competitive strategy that's hard to imitate.

- **Elevate and sustain relevance** by dialing up their agility to align with and collaboratively create solutions that impact their customers' most critical clinical/technical, business and financial priorities, unmet needs, and "CareAbouts." Importantly, customer expectations are shifting fast—and there is little tolerance for "telling me what I already know" or not being highly relevant.

- **Strengthen, expand, and deepen strategic relationships**, moving well beyond "preferred supplier" status to being seen as trusted co-innovators and business advisors.

- **Create and sustain mutual value beyond the product** by developing new revenue streams, developing new business models, reducing costs, and improving efficiencies. Paradoxically, leading companies find that as they create value beyond the core product, sales of core products and services increase.[2] Also, by quantifying and communicating value beyond the product, companies counter commoditization and price pressure. While price remains important, it need not be the only factor.

- **Innovate more effectively** by bringing new-to-company ideas, capabilities, and insights that result in new products, services, and solutions.

- **Mitigate risks inherent in traditional innovation** by reducing market access and demand uncertainty.

- **Accelerate entry into new markets.**

- **Expand value and impact** by replicating, cascading, and scaling to other customers and new accounts.

As one respondent in the SAMA "Report on Current Trends and Practices in Strategic Account Management" put it, "Only a true customer-focused approach that unites and aligns our company's resources on co-value creation for both parties can differentiate us and sustain our growth in the medium to longer term. It's also an approach that can dissolve internal barriers along the way, if strongly led by the CEO downwards."[3]

---

2   Technology companies refer to this as the "attach rate"—the incremental core-product sales generated as a result of bringing new solutions and services to market.

3   Verbatim comment from 2014 "Report on Current Trends and Practices in Strategic Account Management," © Strategic Account Management Association (SAMA), April 2014

Ultimately, creating joint solutions is about increasing customer value and accelerating and sustaining profitable growth, which fuels the lifeblood of business. As compelling as the logic may be, though, creating joint solutions can be one of the toughest strategies to execute.

Creating joint solutions is the collaborative development and deployment of new products, services, solutions, processes, and/or business models that impact mutually prioritized opportunities to create value, differentiation, and profitable growth for the company, the company's customers, and the customer's customer.

"Joint Solution Development, Co-Creation, and Reaching Agreement" is a core SAM competency[4] as defined in SAMA's SAM Competency Model and draws on critical skills essential for high-performance strategic account management.

Figure 13   Joint Solution Development, Co-Creation and Reaching Agreement is a critical SAM competency—as defined in SAMA's SAM Competency Model

Opportunities for creating joint solutions span from incremental improvement of existing products and services to creating new-to-the world solutions, developing new business models, and entering new markets.

---

4   In the SAMA competency model, the Joint Solution Development, Co-Creation and Reaching Agreement competency is defined thusly: "Ability to communicate credibly and effectively at the customer CxO level, demonstrating understanding of the customer's financials and financial strategy. Provides thought-leadership on customer's business issues and priorities, uncovers and validates key challenges. Engages the customer in the account planning process and works collaboratively to identify value-based solutions. Co-creates in areas of highest joint potential and innovation. Quantifies the differential solution/value proposition vis-à-vis competitors demonstrating mutual ROI. Sells high and wide throughout the customer organization—managing Procurement and multilevel relationships with the support and coordination of the account team. Negotiates and reaches agreement on company engagement and specific deals, specifying resource commitment and allocations internally and at the customer."

It is our belief that value may be co-created at three levels of product/service, business model, and market opportunity:

- **Core:** with existing products and services, in existing markets

- **Adjacent:** entering and extending with new-to-company and/or new-to-customer products and markets

- **New:** new-to-the-world products and services, business models, markets, and customers

Figure 14   Opportunities for creating joint solutions span from incremental improvements of existing solutions to new-to-the world solutions, business models and processes

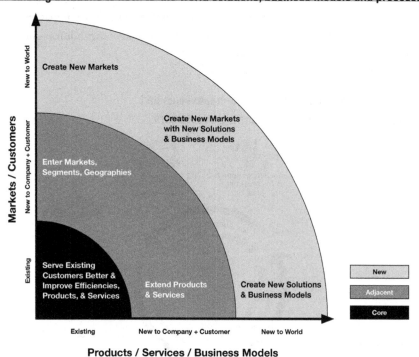

Creating joint solutions is not traditional large account selling. It's something we do *with*, not *to*, the customer.

The hallmark operating principles for effectively creating joint solutions are:

- Outside-in thinking

- Focus on the customer's customer

- High levels of collaboration, transparency, and trust

- Business alignment and mutual prioritization of opportunities

- Value creation and business impact for both the company and the customer

- Joint resourcing and decision making

- Senior-level leader support and sponsorship
- Balancing creative, strategic thinking with disciplined execution
- Leveraging relevant strengths and capabilities of both organizations
- An agile, iterative process enabled by continued feedback and learning

Leading companies who excel at collaboratively creating value with their customers are not trying to do a thousand things well. With clear purpose, and through deliberate practice, they focus on developing the critical capabilities that enable an iterative, flexible process; agile execution; and continuous learning.

While there is no universal template or guaranteed recipe for success, based on The Summit Group's research, benchmarking, and our work with some of the world's top companies, we've distilled what the best do differently to the ten "greatest hits"—i.e., distinctive capabilities—aligned with, and enabling, the collaborative value-creation framework:

Figure 15   What the best do differently to co-create value and develop joint solutions with strategic customers

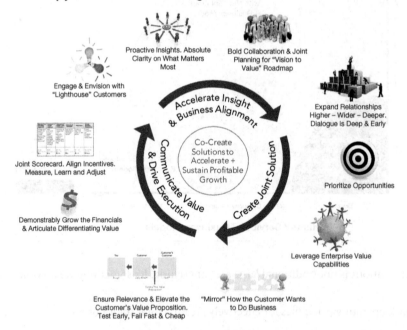

Insight and business alignment:

1. Engage and envision with "lighthouse" customers

2. Develop proactive insights and absolute clarity on what matters most

3. Collaborate boldly and plan jointly for a "Vision to Value" roadmap

4. Expand relationships higher, wider, deeper for a proactive dialogue[5]

5. Prioritize mutual opportunities

Create joint solutions:

6. Leverage enterprise capabilities beyond the product

7. "Mirror" how the customer wants to do business, forming joint-action teams

Communicate value and drive execution:

8. Ensure relevance and elevate the customer's value proposition. Test concepts early, and fail fast and at the lowest cost.

9. Demonstrably grow the financials and articulate differentiating value

10. Create a joint scorecard. Align incentives. Measure and communicate results. Learn and adjust, adjust, adjust.

These "next practices" enable leading companies to discover, understand, and validate the customer's key value drivers, a deep understanding of which maximizes the potential for co-creating value, ensures efficient resource allocation, elevates relationships, differentiates how you show up, and counters competition. An underlying and recurring theme in every successful co-value creation initiative we've been privileged to be a part of over the past 21 years is "trust-based collaboration." What can we learn from this insight?

When deciding with whom to collaborate, leading companies go beyond traditional criteria to assess prospects for strategic business partnerships[6] and look closely at the attributes and behaviors of highly collaborative organizations—as well as poorly collaborating ones. Along with the openness to innovate and being seen as a leader in the industry, these indicators of trust-based collaboration guide us to engage with customers with whom we are most likely to succeed and help us to avoid the pain, costs, and ramifications of failed attempts.

Trust is earned, and it's based on the one party's confidence in the other's capability, transparency, and commitment to consistently deliver and follow through on commitments.[7]

The table in Figure 16 contrasts attributes we've observed that indicate an organization's capacity to build and sustain trust-based collaborative relationships versus those that do not. Those organizations demonstrating the least collaborative behaviors may be good customers, but they may not be the best candidates for co-creating solutions.

---

5 The Oxford Dictionary defines the word *dialogue* as "a discussion between two or more people or groups, especially one directed toward exploration of a particular subject or resolution of a problem."

6 ASAP, Association of Strategic Alliance Partnerships

7 Suggested reading: *The Speed of Trust*, Stephen Covey and *The Trust Edge*, David Horsager

Figure 16   Attributes of the most, and least, collaborative relationships

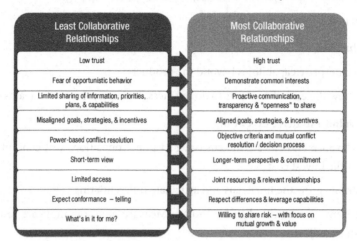

Introducing a framework for creating joint solutions

In this section, we bring you the "how"—a pragmatic, proven operating framework, principles, and tools for creating joint solutions with your strategic customers. There's no "silver bullet" or prescriptive process that gets you from A to Z. An iterative, agile application of a structured yet flexible approach that provides "freedom in a framework" has proven to enable effective execution and to accelerate results. This proposed co-value creation approach is validated in real-world application and is based on the experience of leading companies across industries. Theory does not pay the bills.

Figure 17   A framework for creating joint solutions

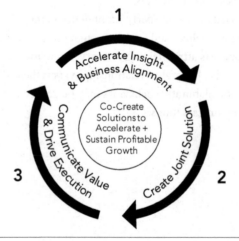

The operating framework we propose for creating joint solutions has three phases: (1) accelerate insight and business alignment, (2) create joint solutions, and (3) communicate value and drive execution.

In the complex business-to-business environment of strategic account management, where no two co-creation opportunities are likely to follow the same path, a prescriptive, robotic, linear process will not accommodate the variability, adaptation, and creativity required for success. Rather, the creating joint solutions framework provides structure to our thinking, secures focus on what matters most, stimulates creativity, and guides our iterative action towards the outcomes we seek—allowing for the dexterity, agility, and flexibility required to navigate the multifaceted dynamics of two (or more) organizations seeking to collaboratively co-create value.

Companies adapt and integrate this framework into their organization's culture and way-of-working to differentiate how they engage and drive growth with their customers. The collaborative co-creation journey becomes an important part of their overall value proposition and competitiveness by creating an exceptional customer experience. Let's walk through each phase to understand what works—the mindset, skill set, and core principles and tools required to create joint solutions with strategic customers.

Phase 1: Accelerate insight and business alignment

In this phase the company and customer:

- Establish mutual intent and guiding principles[8] to collaborate, beyond the transactional relationship, in the discovery and evaluation of opportunities to create new sources of value
- Accelerate and deepen insights into their value-chain drivers—thinking outside-in and looking beyond the product/service to identify major "CareAbouts" (i.e., issues, opportunities, unmet needs, and pain points impacting their business ecosystem) to avoid "product glaucoma"[9]
- Listen louder to the voice of the customer's customer
- Engage in dialogue with relevant stakeholders beyond traditional contact points to extend and validate insights
- Mutually prioritize what matters most, aligning on opportunities and initiatives that are likely to have the greatest impact on end-user value and on each organization's business, considering feasibility and competitive differentiation

At the outcome of this phase, both organizations have identified big "CareAbouts" and prioritized joint opportunities to co-create mutual value. During this phase, leading practitioners reorder their thinking, starting with their customer's customer, to understand why they select one product, service, or solution over another—and to determine what they seek and care about most.

Third Box Thinking™, CareAbouts, joint opportunity prioritization, Value Enablers™, and building compelling value propositions

Third Box Thinking is a principle that operationalizes value co-creation by reordering and aligning how we think, enabling the shift from traditional selling, which starts with product/service features and benefits, to focus on value-chain drivers before considering what we can bring. In our experience, the inside-out, product-centric mindset is one of the hardest things to change, especially when you

---

8   May also be referred to as "rules of engagement," charter, or "intent to collaborate."

9   WebMD defines *glaucoma* as a "progressive vision condition that can lead to permanent blindness."

have historically enjoyed product success. Third Box Thinking begins with the customer's customer (see Figure 18), re-structuring thinking from right to left—starting with deep insight and understanding of what the end-user customers care about/seek, what customers do to deliver value to their customers, and what the company can provide. It's about reverse engineering relevance and listening beyond the product.

Figure 18   Third Box Thinking—a principle and tool enabling companies to listen beyond the product and identify value drivers from the customer's customer's perspective

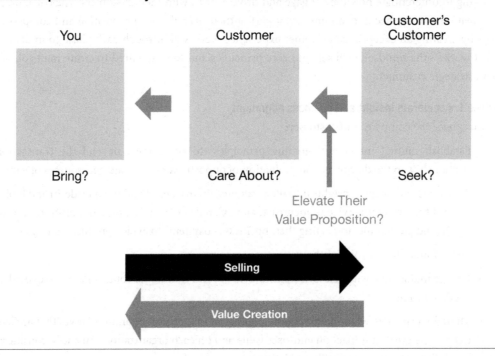

Leading companies gain deep, unique, strategic, and tactical insight into industry value drivers and the customer's business issues, initiatives, and critical success factors. While quantitative and qualitative research and customer satisfaction surveys provide plentiful data, it is usually filtered through third parties, difficult to interpret, harder to act on, and unlikely to provide the depth of insight required to guide co-development of differentiated, customized solutions. Co-value creation places a premium on understanding the "ultimate truth": the unfiltered voice of the customer and of key players along the value chain.

Gaining deeper insight into value drivers requires understanding the "why behind the what." By repeatedly asking "why," we uncover the root cause and expose implications of CareAbouts. The CareAbouts grid prompts probing questions—What? Why? Who?—enabling us to avoid making assumptions and ensuring we dig deeper to understand the "why behind the what."

Clarity, making choices, and focus are crucial to successfully creating joint solutions. Collaborating companies proactively agree on the approach and criteria to prioritize where they will invest resources (time, energy, people, and money) and, importantly, to decide where they will not invest.

We propose a simple framework to guide collaborative prioritization of opportunities for creating joint solutions. The joint opportunity prioritization tool enables understanding of the "fit" between company and the customer's strategic agenda, and guides us to assess the feasibility, scope, competitive differentiation, and relative importance of the opportunity itself. This framework provides questions that can be used to screen, evaluate, and prioritize where to play and how to focus on what matters most.

Joint opportunity prioritization is based on answers to four strategic questions:

1. **Impact:** If we were to invest in creating a solution for this opportunity, can we have a meaningful impact on what the customer and customer's customer (end-user) care about most?

2. **Attractiveness:** If we were to invest, do we expect this to be good business (aligned with our vision, goals, and strategy) that generates a satisfactory return for our organization?

3. **Feasibility:** Do we have the capabilities, competencies, time, capital/budget/funding, resources, and support to create and execute? What is the likelihood of us being successful?

4. **Differentiation:** If we were to invest in creating a solution for this opportunity, can we win? Will this solution positively distinguish us in our marketplace, or are we merely investing to be at parity with competitive options?

Figure 19   Joint opportunity prioritization

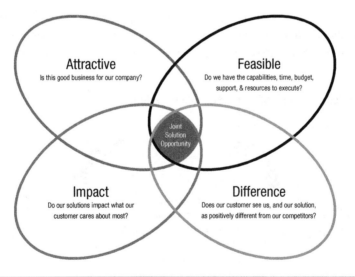

To advance on the creating joint solutions journey, it's essential to secure business alignment between, and within, each company. In this regard, we always hear the biggest obstacles come from within.[10]

Based on deep insights, prioritization of opportunities, and cross-business alignment, we move to the next phase.

---

10 This insight is validated by SAMA's "2014 Report on Current Trends and Practices in SAM" where two of the three top challenges facing effective SAMs were (a) "Enabling SAMs to collaborate internally to align resources for the customers" and (b) "SAMs struggle to identify and develop long-term growth opportunities as opposed to just focusing on short-term objectives."

Phase 2: Create joint solutions

In this phase, the company and customer:

- Agree on and apply an approach to creating joint solutions that leverage the enterprise resources, capabilities, enablers, and relative strengths of each organization

- Collaboratively engage in structured ideation and brainstorming to identify "beyond-the-product/service" enablers and generate potential solutions—drawing on relevant resources and strong capabilities from across both enterprises

- Screen solutions and enablers for inclusion, exclusion, or further development considering their relevance, impact, and feasibility.

- Align, engage, and commit relevant resources to develop the prioritized solution(s)

- Value engineer to optimize the solution for impact and differentiation—considering solution components and enablers that can be added, eliminated, elevated, or reduced

- Prototype and test the solution—with emphasis on agile development[11]: testing early and failing fast, at the lowest cost

At the outcome of this phase, both organizations have co-created a joint solution relevant to the prioritized opportunity and have agreed to move ahead to build and validate the business case, communicate compelling value, and to pilot and then implement the solution, joint initiative, or new business model.

Our proposed approach for creating joint solutions starts with—and focuses on—a prioritized customer "CareAbout," aligns relevant products and services, and integrates enterprise capabilities beyond the core product/service that impact what the customer and/or end-user cares about most.

Figure 20   A structured approach for creating joint solutions

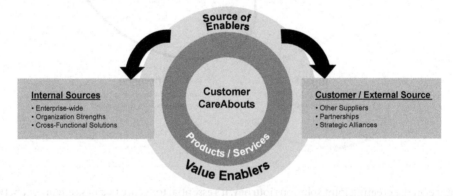

Central to successfully creating joint solutions is the ability of each collaborating organization to leverage their enterprise-wide capabilities. Value enablers are any asset, capability, company strength, or resource beyond the core product or service offering. While the idea of drawing on relevant

---

11 "Agile development is an alternative to traditional project management, typically used in software development. It helps teams respond to unpredictability through incremental, iterative work cadences, known as sprints. Agile methodologies are an alternative to waterfall, or traditional sequential development." *Source: http://agilemethodology.org/*

cross-business, enterprise resources to co-create solutions with strategic customers sounds logical, fundamental, and simple, in our experience it's not always easy—and not common practice.

For many co-creation initiatives, this is where the "rubber meets the road": when the joint solutions team engages and requests relevant resources, beyond the product, from across the business. To facilitate access to solution enablers and support their integration into new, "beyond-the-product" offerings, we suggest the following:

- Ensure executive-level support and communication of the "grander why"—why creating value with strategic customers is central to your company's strategy and success.

- Engage and align the "critical crowd"—i.e., relevant internal stakeholders—early in the creating joint solutions journey, well before you make a specific request to invest their, or their team's, time and resources.

- Build a comprehensive list and categorize enabling capabilities around core value themes such as reducing cost, improving efficiencies, growing revenue, and elevating the customer experience.

- Identify customer and company gaps in capabilities—i.e., value enablers that are missing yet critical to co-creating value. Determine if these are capabilities you can build, buy, or source elsewhere.

- Identify and engage "owners" of key value enablers—using the customer's voice to articulate why these capabilities/resources are important, the impact on the customer's business, the value to the company, the cost of inaction, the joint solutions roadmap, and what matters next.

- Leverage relevant enablers to co-create solutions using structured brainstorming and creative design thinking[12] to generate concepts and potential solutions.

- Move forward to prototype, test, and refine your solution.

Phase 3: Communicate value and drive execution

In this phase, the company and customer:

- Develop their business case and compelling customer value proposition

- Establish and execute their plan to deploy the joint solution/initiative

- Agree on a governance framework, project plan, scorecard and review cadence to drive joint initiatives forward, faster

- Reflect to capture lessons learned, build on what's working, and assess opportunities to adjust strategy and scale solutions

At the outcome of this phase, the compelling, differentiating value proposition and business case for the co-developed solution have been quantified and clearly articulated, the joint solution has been launched, and a plan has been agreed upon to scale and roll out to other customers or markets.

Quantifying and communicating compelling, differentiating value to key stakeholders within the customer's organization, and to the customer's customer, is fundamental and essential to the practice of co-creating value. Ultimately, if the value of your solution is not recognized, believed in, and

---

12 Design thinking is central to creating joint solutions by focusing first on defining the problem/unmet need/opportunity, and then implementing the solution, always with the needs of the user demographic at the core of concept development.

accounted for, your company will not be able to capture and realize the value co-created in the joint solutions process.

Value propositions are a well-established, yet often poorly practiced, concept in sales and marketing. Through research[13] we've established that less than 10 percent of customers see their suppliers "creating real value, and being worthy of a long-term strategic relationship." As one customer commented on their supplier's value proposition, "This sounds like brochure-speak."

We need to ask ourselves the question, "Why do value propositions seldom resonate?" Based on our research and work with clients, we've established that compelling value propositions resonate because they: focus on what matters most to the customer; clearly articulate the differentiating value of your solution, compared to the best alternative; are quantified in the customer's currency; and provide evidence of impact and proof of your company's ability to deliver.

Figure 21   Characteristics of compelling value propositions that resonate

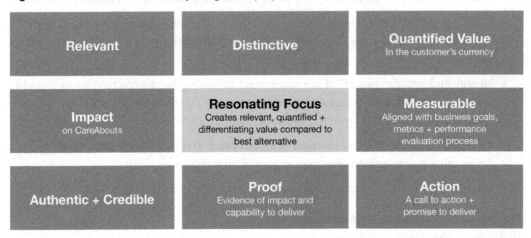

We suggest a simple Value Creation Framework™ to collaboratively develop your compelling, relevant, quantified, and differentiating value proposition. The framework provides a non-prescriptive structure for communicating thought. It enables authentic articulation of your joint solution's impact on the customer's top "CareAbouts." This framework, structured around four words—them, us, fit, and proof—assures relevance and resonance by aligning what you bring (i.e., your solution) with the customer's major needs and priorities.

Them: What do they care about? We need to truly understand what our customers care about. What keeps them up at night? What are their key issues and concerns? What is important to them? How are they measured, paid, and rewarded?

Us: What do we have? Here's where you articulate relevant products, services, and value enablers. What pertinent capabilities and assets can you bring, beyond and/or wrapped around core products and services?

---

13 Strategic Sales Effectiveness Research—The Summit Group, Consalia, ITC, London Business School, "What Customers Seek," 2008–2014

Fit: How does what you have impact what's important to the customer and customer's customer? Quantify and describe the impact of your solution on the key issues, concerns, and value drivers of your customer and customer's customer. Articulate your solution's difference compared to the next best alternative.

Proof: Prove it! Provide the examples and evidence of the value you will bring and demonstrate proof that you can deliver and execute.

Applying this framework guides us to create, articulate, and quantify customer-centric value propositions that resonate and enable the company and customer to realize value created through the joint solutions process.

What matters next

While our proposed framework for creating joint solutions is simple—and it's meant to be—what distinguishes leading companies from their competition is how they institutionalize this approach. From our experience, companies that outperform their peers in implementing creating joint solutions do the following:

- Establish a replicable enterprise-wide approach to customer-centric co-value creation. The whole organization—not only sales and marketing—is oriented towards the customer. At Cisco, for example, CEO John Chambers made sure the primary focus was on the customer at a time when other vendors were focused on technology. Customer satisfaction is a company-wide performance metric enabled by cross-functional teams, account segmentation, executive sponsorship, customer advisory boards, and a world-class customer relationship development process.

- Continually refine which customers they choose to align with and focus resources on. Strategic fit, market attractiveness, and trust-based collaboration criteria must enter into the selection process. The Summit Group believes it is essential to identify, in addition to strategic customers, "lighthouse" companies who are forward-thinking innovators prepared to share risk and resources, and who are expected to drive future segment growth. These may or may not be current customers.

- Take collaboration to the next level to secure alignment, gain deeper insight into customer priorities, and uncover new mutual growth opportunities that often would have been invisible to each company acting on its own. In one Bain trend study,[14] more than 65 percent of the executive respondents believed they could dramatically boost innovation by collaborating with outsiders, even competitors.

- Rigorously prioritize opportunities and bring clarity to where there is fit—and where there is not.

- Articulate a compelling value proposition, which aligns self-interest with customer priorities and quantifies internal and customer outcomes.

---

14 "Tools & Trends Study" based on response from 1,221 international executives, Bain Co.

- Effectively act on strategic customer and value-chain insights to co-create relevant, differentiated solutions that leverage their mutual cross-enterprise capabilities and resources. As Jack Welch put it, "An organization's ability to learn, and translate that learning into action rapidly, is the ultimate competitive advantage."[15]

- Secure mutual commitment between company and customer as well as internally—through joint planning, common scorecards, and reviews—to drive effective go-to-market execution and enable constant learning.

- Elevate the account team's mindset and skill set by building core relationship development skills and leveraging team members' signature strengths. The application of these skills and strengths is reinforced through authentic sales leadership and coaching.

This summarizes more than 20 years of The Summit Group's collaboration with leading companies in the pragmatic pursuit, deliberate practice, and real-world application of the co-value creation framework and principles reviewed. We are often asked, "What's the 'silver bullet' to co-creating value?" Our response, and recommendation, is this: "Just do it!" By developing and institutionalizing enterprise-wide competencies to create joint solutions, leading companies are able to have significant immediate and long-term impact on customer loyalty, profit, value, and growth.

---

15 Jack Welch, former Chairman & CEO, General Electric

Chapter 14

The most important element for managing the multifunctional team is the leadership abilities of the SAM. In the present chapter, Mercuri International, an expert in global customer management, will discuss the capabilities and the duties of a SAM to effectively manage a global customer. To summarize the most important facets of SAM leadership, I would say the SAM as a leader needs to have a clear strategic vision for the customer, he or she needs to have the ability to effectively communicate that vision, both internally and to the key customer stakeholders, and he or she needs to make sure that the metrics are in place to effectively drive the customer value process, holding people accountable for delivering to the customer's needs. The SAM also must have the leadership acumen to assemble the right team and to ensure the necessary customer alignment to deliver on the value proposition. This has led some experts to call the SAM a political entrepreneur, which speaks to the SAM's ability to lead teams, navigate the customer, and manage his or her internal organization for optimal results. (Bernard Quancard)

Mobilizing and Leading Multifunctional Teams

By Robert F. Box
Partner
Mercuri International

It's a beautiful Friday afternoon. You're wrapping up a busy, productive week; you made it through without any calamities or unusual concerns. Now you're looking forward to unwinding this weekend—two days with the family, a dinner with friends, and even some rare down time. You might start that biography of John Adams you've been meaning to read...

Then at 4:50 p.m., the phone rings. Your customer in Brussels is on the line, and he is incensed about developments at his manufacturing plant in a country seven time zones away. It gets worse: You learn that one of your account team members stationed near the plant knew about the situation two weeks ago. Not only did he neglect to inform you, but he also didn't mention it to your customer, whose outrage is clear. "What is your team doing over there, anyway?" he practically screams into the phone. "Don't you communicate in your company? You need to solve this now!"

Quickly, you call a meeting about legal issues and angles involved in your contract with this customer and possible consequences of not fulfilling all the terms. You call your colleague in Belgium only to find his weekend has already started and he's in a restaurant at a family birthday party. In the meantime, emails from across the pond are piling up. Your weekend turns out to be anything but restful; you spend the entire time worrying about your options and making things right with the Brussels emergency. The entire next week unfolds at the same hectic, panicky pace. When the crisis finally is over, you ask yourself, "What have I really accomplished, and did I lead my team—or did they lead me?"

This is a typical day in the life of a swamped strategic or global account manager. It's a role that is complex and demanding, and it involves leading without line authority across functions, divisions, and geographic regions. In this chapter, we will examine the specifics of leading and managing multifunctional teams.

My experience in managing international sectors spans several decades, so I'm in a good position to write this chapter. I've worked in the United States and also spent about 20 years based in Europe, working with global companies based in North America, Europe, and Asia.

We know that creating value for the customer involves many steps, all of which are covered elsewhere in this book. This chapter will speak to improving the functionality of the global team in order to develop and deliver on the value proposition, and we'll use Wacker Chemie AG, a worldwide chemical company founded in 1914, as a case study. I have worked with Wacker for years, helping them develop some of the strategies and processes discussed here.

Wacker operates around the world and employs a team of SAMs who must be effective across the globe. To that end, Wacker considers these key areas when they want to improve the account manager's function:

- Interpersonal skills

- Strategic leadership

- Global perspective

- Measurement of SAM

Each of these areas has multiple dimensions, and we will look closely at them all.

Interpersonal skills

Communication is a key element in every account manager's success. It's the vehicle for building trust between colleagues, and between SAMs and customers. Wacker utilizes internal tools for clear strategic communication about each account, which is useful both within the core team and for communicating with executives.

Some of the company's practices in communicating effectively are common sense. Wacker aims, for one thing, to conduct all meetings in English, no matter where they are held or who will attend. Some of these meetings might take place in China, and no doubt the managers in that part of Asia would prefer that Chinese be spoken at meetings. But that would mean others in attendance, and those who are affected by what transpires at the meetings, wouldn't be able to talk about what happens or act on any decisions made there. Hiring translators takes time, and it's easier all around—and more inclusive—if only English is spoken. This also prevents managers from one locale from exerting more influence than others simply because of a linguistic advantage. Most companies don't have a specific system, spelled out in writing, for communications; but Wacker recognized the importance of communicating effectively and made it one of its so-called Golden Rules, which I'll explain at length in the "Global Perspective" section below.

Only with good communications can global managers, line managers, and customers build trust, which is a vital ingredient for effectively conducting business. It would be nice if trust building could always be an organic process, but when it's left to chance, personalities can get in the way. So Wacker has systemized trust building. One tactic is requiring account managers to hold face-to-face meetings with their teams, which reinforces the idea that physical distance doesn't have to mean social distance. Wacker goes out of its way to make sure managers regard their teams as one entity—not (for example) six French, three Chinese, two Americans, and three South Africans. The team is the team, acting in tandem as one.

When it comes to building trust, the little things count. Thanking people for their help, congratulating them on a job well done, or involving them in decisions can go a long way toward motivating and aligning with them—whether you're interacting with a customer, a fellow SAM, or the most junior member of your team. Asking for feedback shows people that you respect their expertise and opinions. And be sure not to "over manage." Giving colleagues the space to disagree with each other without you stepping in or shutting them down can encourage honest, forward-looking communication throughout the company.

One other obvious-seeming but often overlooked facet of team building is the art of small talk, especially if your team is geographically dispersed. Don't be afraid to coach on this. And by small talk, I don't mean empty, time-wasting chitchat. I mean conversation that's more personal than business discussions—the other person's background, what they like most about living in a certain city, whether they found it easy to learn a second language, and the like. Teach your account team members to make their questions open ended and to listen for areas of common ground or shared interests. If you can make these habits second nature, you'll notice that trust begins to build organically.

Strategic leadership

One challenge the account managers at Wacker face is moving from an operational to a strategic mindset, though this challenge is, of course, hardly unique to Wacker. At Wacker they strive to prevent problems before they happen by building a company culture that's proactive, rather than reactive. And because the SAM is perceived as the authority, the leader with ability and smarts, he or she needs to be the most proactive of all.

The focus on proactivity depends on devising a detailed account plan, which relies on the use of "action sheets" to drive behaviors. For instance, an objective might be to visit a customer in India with a new formulation within the next six months. The action sheet items related to this objective might include:

- Work with the lab on the formulation

- Get a timeline from the lab

- Meet with the procurement people on your team

- Decide on whether to increase the price and if so, by how much

- Run your account plan by others on your team and get their feedback as to which items are realistic and advantageous, and which need adjusting

Some action sheet items will be assigned to global team members, while some will be handled locally. But planning ahead in this way, and sharing the planned actions with the entire team, leaves much less to chance and will free up time that would otherwise be spent putting out fires. But beware: If you focus only on the tasks at hand, it's easy to lose sight of the overall account vision. So SAMs need to be able to:

- Detect patterns
- Look beyond the details and day-to-day issues
- Visualize the "bigger picture"—where you want to go and how you will get there as a team

At Wacker it starts with team leadership, which starts with giving account managers the authority to work both within their teams and to align their teams with the rest of the organization. To this end, it can be helpful to bring together people who perform different functions within the company. Consider holding a retreat for your team where someone from accounting, a lab technician, and a marketing person (just for instance) all present the challenges their departments face and plans for overcoming them. At Wacker, personnel from across the company often participate in the SAM development program, often as coaches and line managers.

Wacker facilitates this multifunctional sharing both in two-day facilitated sessions and in periodic "fireside chats." Seeing how all the moving parts operate in tandem can get "firefighters" thinking more strategically and help them avoid getting snagged on day-to-day coordination. Awareness of other departments is vital to optimal functioning, and Wacker tries to create that mutual, interactive awareness not only for global account teams but across the entire organization.

Many companies create strong value propositions for their customers, but unless they're able to maximize their own internal relationships and resources—which requires deep knowledge and awareness across their organization—they're going to fail to deliver on their promises. Wacker pushes its SAMs to promote and endorse personal connections because, in reality, all business is personal. Whenever possible, managers are encouraged to give instructions or feedback via web conferences and phone calls, rather than by email.

Silos aren't going anywhere any time soon. But when they're united by a common vision, and when departments communicate with each other, planners and managers can innovate more easily.

Global perspective

A company's culture can heavily impact the success of a strategic relationship. How informed are the people on your team regarding the cultures involved in this account—and not only the cultures of their own colleagues and customer contacts, but all those across the entire ecosystem?

In simple terms, adopting a "global perspective" means having the ability to adapt and work effectively anywhere. One of the most fundamental concepts in evolving the account manager's global perspective (and that of the global team) is "high context" versus "low context" communication. The concept of high- and low-context communication was developed not by a business guru but by an anthropologist named Edward T. Hall. Low-context communication revolves around sharing concise bits of information with little background or context needed. High-context communication requires the speaker to impart much more background and context.

Traditionally, most Americans communicate in a "low context" manner. But if you are working with an account manager in India or France, for instance—countries where the communicator is likely to explain everything he or she can about the situation at hand, even though the manager in the United States may want just the headline—then the quality of their communications (and, thus, their relationship) may weaken.

These two communication styles also affect people's physical reactions during conversation. In high-context cultures, reactions are very reserved; people don't tend to show their emotions as expressively as we do in the United States. Even the notion of time is different in high- and low-context cultures. In low-context cultures, time is much more flexible. In high-context cultures, agendas and work are highly organized and planned to the smallest detail. These are all things account managers need to keep in mind, both in terms of their own global teams and their global customers.

High or low context is evident, too, in the ways in which business people prepare to speak. In Eastern Asia, for instance, managers are likely to prepare at length before they give a talk or even share their perspectives with colleagues. But in the United States, independent thinking and quick decisions are often valued over careful deliberation.

Like all cultural differences, any clash between high- and low-context colleagues from different cultures is easy to avoid by learning how your team members working and living in other cultures are accustomed to operating and by being ready to adjust your own approach accordingly.

Another major factor in developing a global perspective is how you define when a situation is merely a challenge to work through versus when it has become a problem that needs to be solved. In the United States we enjoy a culture of entrepreneurship, what some call a "can-do" attitude. In situations where there's been an operational hiccup, a U.S.-based team may see an opportunity for improvement that ultimately strengthens the overall customer-supplier relationship, while an Asia-based team might see something "broken" in need of fixing.

These different perspectives, and the kinds of responses they call for, all came into play in the anecdote at the beginning of this chapter. Remember: You're in the hot seat because your account team member didn't inform you of the complications developing in your customer's plant because he saw the apparent logistics problem as a new reality that he and the team would cope with and work through; he didn't think the issue warranted escalation. Your customer, on the other hand, viewed the issue as a dire problem that needed to be fixed right away. They each looked at it from their own cultural perspectives.

These different cultural perspectives can create challenges for global teams—but notice I said "challenges," not "problems." By simply being aware of the possible differences, and communicating and working more closely, potential blow-ups like the one I described can be avoided.

Inevitably, global operations have stakeholders operating in a high-context culture. One way of acknowledging and catering to this cultural preference is to send a detailed agenda in advance of any meeting and to follow up with minutes afterwards. It's a basic action that can accomplish much in terms of collegial relationships.

For each strategic account, Wacker's SAMs develop a list of approaches they call "Golden Rules," which enshrines transcending of cultural differences as an official account policy. The Golden Rules are created with the team and the account manager as a way to formalize how they will work together across the customer organization. For example, one rule might spell out when managers should start talking about a challenge and when they need to escalate to a higher level. It's a very clear process addressing such issues as the best ways to handle value propositions, testing, and pricing. Essentially, it lays out how the team should cooperate, no matter where they are in the world.

To give one example, Wacker has a defined process around purchasing. Managers are to refer to Wacker's account-agreed pricing approach and to consult colleagues; if Wacker develops and releases a new product or solution during the year, a specific process for offering that product, overseen by the SAM, is already carved in stone.

To further breed cultural awareness across teams, Wacker arranges national and global meetings. In addition to SAMs, line managers and others are invited to attend and given extra travel days to accommodate core team members.

Wacker understands that if it's going to do business globally, it needs to take a more global approach and hire leaders from Asia, Europe, and the United States. Sometimes global team members are going to bump into local customs, and having managers from across the globe helps establish culturally sensitive approaches to work practice.

Measuring outcomes

It's not easy to directly measure improvements in leadership. However, Wacker did create an internal measurement system for SAMs based on how a manager's team has influenced revenues and profit margins. The account manager is responsible for following through on any recommendations.

The company uses a mix of metrics in these reviews, including:

- **Is the team working with the right contacts at the account?** The most productive connections will fit the team's objectives. Sometimes that means establishing contacts at the executive level, sometimes it means connecting with a mid-level manager or technical liaison. It's the SAM's job to know the account in sufficient detail to zero in on the best decision maker for whatever the team needs to accomplish and to align the team to foster the interaction.

- **Does the SAM understand the customer's decision-making process?** Every account is bound to be complex, and the account manager needs to know the specifics of each customer's process. What steps are involved in its purchasing system? What's its research methodology? How will the customer assess its success in working with the account team? Will the company be looking for any red flags that the account team should avoid?

- **What is the account team's corporate communication process?** Are the account managers carrying the right messages to the customer? Is the team using communication tools in a good way? How does the team present the value proposition?

- **Are account team members leveraging their product range in a way that will benefit their customers?** Customers engage suppliers because they believe the supplier's team members are the experts and can show them how to boost their own profitability. The account manager should be able to see how his or her own team members are demonstrating to their customers the value of the relationship.

- **What is the account team's approach toward innovation with the customer?** Is the team discussing innovation with the right person to make it happen? How well is the customer implementing its joint plans with the team for innovation? Are the account team and the customer working well together to innovate both their products and processes? Do they see eye-to-eye when it comes to making changes?

Some of these items may seem like a given, but for many companies it's the basics that trip them up. They may need an outsider such as the SAM to simply show them a blueprint for moving forward.

It's not a hard metric, but every year Wacker's global SAMs get feedback from their own teams. The company creates a spider graph to show each team's year-to-year progress—how the account team has evolved and how the SAM can improve. And every year or two, Wacker collects feedback from the SAMs themselves as part of its aim for continuous improvement.

Based on several years of collecting the above measurements, Wacker strongly suspects that the success of the account team in the above metrics correlates strongly with the long-term success of an account.

Conclusion

Every day is busy in the SAM's world. Those who do an "average" job are capable global coordinators. But those who have moved from reactive firefighting to being proactive enablers of success become global strategic leaders. They are the innovators, and they get there by focusing on global perspective, interpersonal skills, and strategic leadership.

Wacker's approach to global team leadership is a work in progress, but these are some of the best practices that have helped them develop a strong approach to leading and managing multifunctional teams. By following the strategies outlined in this chapter, and by measuring and working with both soft and hard data, Wacker has fostered success in delivering value for both its customers and itself.

Chapter 15

Even though the whole purpose of the SAMA SAM Process is to co-create value with your strategic customers, which in turn involves managing multi-stakeholder relationships at your customer, all too often cold hard reality puts you back into the jaws of Procurement and its long-held bias toward price and commoditization. This is why SAMA considers negotiation to be a critical component of managing relationships based on value rather than price. This chapter covers how to change the conversation from price to value and how companies transform negotiation into a hard, rather than a soft, skill. It's amazing what a little knowledge, data, and a very structured, disciplined process can do for flipping the conversation with Procurement from one about price breaks to one about value. (Bernard Quancard)

Nalco: Return on Investment through Negotiation and Closing

By Carrie Welles
Partner
Think! Inc. and 5600 blue

and

James Ford
Global Head of Client Development
Arcadis[16]

In 2008 when the global economic environment produced one of the most competitive markets in history, Nalco's SAM program found itself scrambling to protect the value of each customer solution. This translated into visible, significant business problems, including margins eroding at an unprecedented pace, rising account attrition rates, stalled technology deployment, and new account production. A formal benchmark study on negotiation effectiveness conducted by Think! Inc. identified the following issues as contributing factors. The percentages show Nalco's cross-functional leaders who agreed or significantly agreed with each corresponding statement.

External market factors impacting negotiation were on the rise, such as:

- Procurement was more professional and skilled (100%).

- Customers were more price- and commodity-focused and demanded more concessions (75%).

- The SAM team faced more irrational competitive behavior (75%).

---

16 At the time this chapter was written, Ford was vice president of global strategic accounts at Nalco.

The company's strategic reaction to these market factors was insufficient to meet the market forces, to wit:

- The SAM team's negotiation skills were not on par with procurement counterparts. The company lacked a formal training program for strategic negotiation (100%).

- Account management/sales strategy was strong, but negotiation strategy was a soft skill left to the assigned SAM's individual capability (100%).

- Negotiation decision making was highly centralized, leaving little autonomy in SAMs' hands (92%).

- Cross-functional departments that influenced a deal had their own goals and acted independently. This silo approach was often at odds with achieving optimal outcomes in negotiation (52%).

Nalco's tactical reaction to these market factors was not as aggressive and structured as desired:

- There was no well-defined process for negotiation but a tendency to react using an *ad hoc* approach rather than one that was proactive, fact-based, and systematic (100%).

- There was no well-defined strategy for irrational competitive behavior (100%).

- In exchange for customer demands, the SAM team rarely traded. There was often erosion in Nalco's overall value in a deal (100%).

All those surveyed agreed competency in organizational negotiation was needed to combat market conditions. The company decided to choose a solution that would not only tackle the aforementioned concerns but turn a seemingly soft skill—as negotiation is so often tagged—into a hard skill, which is defined as a business process that is measurable and repeatable. The company set out to build both SAM and organizational competency that would heighten courage, reduce outcome variance, and produce measurable impact one deal at a time.

Building an organizational negotiation strategy

Think! recommended that Nalco move away from a series of training events. To change the culture, this effort needed the horsepower of support from executives serious about implementation who fundamentally understood that success in negotiation did not reside with the SAM team alone. We focused on three areas:

- Gathering all cross-functional stakeholders who either touched or influenced strategic account negotiation to gain common ground on guidelines and parameters for optimal deals

- Introducing a common process by which the SAM team could achieve those optimal results

- Measuring impact and return on investment. Commitment on what and how to measure was gained from cross-functional internal stakeholders spanning executive leadership, key account and sales management, marketing, pricing, operations, finance, legal, and human resources.

With everyone's voice captured we went to work introducing a common framework to consistently prepare for negotiation, incorporating the agreed-upon guidelines and parameters. We defined this effort as building an organizational negotiation strategy.

Executing the strategy through deal-level alignment

The framework began with Think! research from 20-plus years tracking business-to-business street-level negotiation. We know that 97 percent of what happens in a B2B negotiation falls into one of two categories: Customers will either refer to their alternative as better and use that leverage to ask for concessions, or they'll say, "I can get the same thing cheaper somewhere else." Nalco learned three analytical concepts to anticipate and prepare for the "same thing cheaper" conversation, then used data to present offers. We refer to this pragmatic approach as negotiation blueprinting, and it was easily coached, remembered, and integrated upstream into the company's consultative selling process.

1. Consequences of no agreement (CNA)

The most important element in negotiation is proving value. In its absence negotiation focuses on price. The first half of the most common tactic in negotiation globally is "same thing." ("I can get the same thing cheaper.") What Think! refers to as CNA analysis helps remedy this by finding where the proposed solution meets the customer's objectives better than its alternative in a particular negotiation. Nalco's SAM team needed to prove that its solution for every deal was better than the customer's alternative. CNA involves in-depth analysis of the impact on customers from delaying decisions and using a supplier's competitor. The concept allows Nalco's SAMs to identify its real-time value one deal at a time given its customer's needs and the perceived alternative to reaching agreement. Usually the SAM team finds that the customer's stakeholders have inflated perceptions of how compelling the alternative is or stakeholders have bluffed because their alternative is weak. Either way, understanding this concept empowers Nalco's SAMs to more clearly differentiate value and diplomatically educate buyers on true alternatives or tactfully call bluffs—whichever the case dictates.

This analysis became especially critical when contract renewal started with one of the company's largest strategic accounts, a recognized leader in the retail and foodservice industry. Dangerous momentum built as the customer openly compared Nalco to its closest competitor, stating misperceptions that needed to be professionally and delicately addressed. In short the customer thought the company could be replaced, and Nalco had to work to show its customer's internal stakeholders this wasn't going to be so easy. Nalco began its CNA and determined that the following would occur if it lost this customer:

- $7 million in short- and long-term revenue to Nalco from this customer would be lost.
- The competitor would be empowered.
- A key reference would be lost.
- Nalco would no longer be the sole-source supplier. (It had been the incumbent and only supplier.)
- Access to new markets and applications would be lost.
- Nalco would lose access to a total of approximately $15 million in revenue from all affected sources.

Next, the company sized up the customer's CNA and quantified the impact to the extent possible. Highlights included:

- The cost to transition to another supplier = $1 million
- Potential price savings = $500,000
- Management changes at 150 sites = $?
- The loss of a global partner that had delivered past net savings of more than $50 million
- The loss of total-cost-of-ownership projects tagged at $5 million
- Alienating internal supporters = $?
- The risk to production = $?

Though all costs were not completely understood, Nalco's SAM team felt far more empowered and courageous articulating to the customer that changing suppliers would be significantly more painful than staying. The "I can get the same thing" conversation was bypassed; the "cheaper and needing concessions" conversation followed.

2. Trades

Ultimately the concept of trading for something of equal or greater value avoids value-detracting concessions and expands the opportunity for all. This was a good first step in helping the SAM team prevent the loss of value. The team practiced expanding a negotiation's financial pie by adding as many value-creating elements as possible. A more in-depth analysis taught the team how to prioritize and articulate the risks (terms and conditions) and investments (prices) for both sides. Simply put, this concept put direct focus on protecting Nalco's value and getting compensation for the value extracted during CNA analysis. The company achieved this by cataloging and quantifying as many aspects of its value proposition as possible, prioritizing a deal's approved aspects to give ammunition to the SAM team to consistently execute deals with minimal variance. Choosing to protect or give away value within any given deal has become systematic, not muddled. The team now actively looks for trades that are of low cost to Nalco and high value to the customer.

When the customer frequently exerts concession pressure during a negotiation, the company is ready. Thoughtful preparation by the SAM team allows it to organize prioritized trades and anticipate push-back from the customer so its answer is never "No" but "Yes, if ...."

"The prioritized catalog of trades now allows Nalco marketing management to give back autonomy to the SAMs knowing that they understand what they can and cannot offer a customer," says Tony Stanich, Nalco vice president for global corporate accounts.

3. Multiple equal offers (MEOs)

After identifying value and the trades required to be paid for it, the challenge is to change the typical conversation with the customer from product price to solution value. We refer to the concept articulating this as MEOs. It helps the company develop, formalize, and propose in a concise format those business relationships populated with the appropriate trades associated with a particular solution.

The concept sends a flexible, creative message to customers in a world where a sales organization's precedents (and its competitors') usually offer just the opposite. MEO examples are as follows:

- Meet bid specifications to drive down cost.

- Continue the partnership and accelerate innovation and technology.

- Globally expand the partnership through sustainable initiatives for water and energy optimization.

"The MEO format allows us to put structure around the deal and align each one next to each other so the decision makers can visually see the different offerings," Stanich says. "This makes their decision making happen even faster. We are able to tailor each offer to our various decision makers directly—e.g., procurement, engineering, and finance. Because there is a formalized process in place, it has empowered the SAMs and has given them confidence. Early on, there was skepticism about whether this format was going to be effective versus giving the customer one proposal. It has proven to be an outstanding method to bring more value to Nalco and the customer."

Using technology to create a database for negotiation collaboration

Nalco's negotiations are no longer a one-off activity. The SAM team uses a proprietary Think! execution platform customized specifically for the company. The "Nalco value blueprint" software produces collaboration and allows for:

- Quicker information gathering and account team discussion through drop-down informational menus that help combat "the same thing" and "cheaper"

- Cross-functional collaboration, functional leaders and SAM personnel see each deal's whole picture

- Contributions from sales executives, marketing, operations, finance, and legal to execute deal-level trades within approved ranges. This enables sales to negotiate and close the best deal every time and fight the centralized approach to decision making in negotiation.

- Real-time adaptation as the market and the company's solutions evolve

- Improved deal quality whether executing one or 100 deals

"The 'Nalco value blueprint' software gave us the ability to quickly and effectively share our most creative trades and best practices across our company," says James Ford, formerly Nalco's vice president of global strategic accounts. "While embedding the fundamental concepts for use by our key account managers and marketing teams, the tool actually made all best practices readily available at their fingertips. We've found that putting the tool into use maximizes our probability of success in every negotiation we pursue. Without the customized electronic blueprint as an integral part of our deployment plan, Nalco would not have achieved such rapid success in our negotiations and strong payback from our investment."

Results

Two years since implementation the company has shown impressive results. Going back to the events that propelled Nalco to action, success measures have been captured as follows:

- Concepts are embedded in the sales culture as evidenced by the common language and blueprint technology used in negotiation.
- More than $3.2 million in revenue is attributed to the process.
- New technology deployment is up 160 percent from the previous year.
- New account production is up 40 percent from the previous year.
- The win/loss record against the top two competitors was eight to one and 10 to one respectively.

ROI

- The total revenue attributed to the process thus far, including specific revenue-related metrics tracked for each negotiation taken through the blueprint process, is $3.2 million.
- The total investment in the initiative thus far, including travel expenses for meetings and marketing and Think! fees, is $439,000.
- The ROI thus far is 628 percent.
- The payback period was a year.

"Strategic negotiation is purposeful communication," says John Stewart, a Nalco global strategic account manager. "The concepts and knowledge that we've gained through this disciplined process have allowed us to build a well-thought-out negotiation plan every time. We now proactively drive the negotiation, putting choices in front of our customers that make them think and discuss new areas of co-value creation that we have introduced. We are able to stay the course more easily and maintain the integrity of our offers when we use this process. With all opportunities worth winning, these are principles we will apply."

Chapter 16

The sixth step in the co-value creation process revolves around executing on value. We agree wholeheartedly with customers when they say that executing on value is a prerequisite for a long-lasting relationship. Without seamless, smooth execution, there will be no collaborative co-value creation and nothing on which to build a durable long-term relationship.

In the chapter that follows, Dennis Chapman uses examples from his own basketball and business careers to illustrate the key conditions necessary for successful execution. As always, you have to create a virtuous circle by which you execute, you measure, you fine tune the execution, and then you measure some more. Furthermore, the author sagely illustrates how relationships and mutual commitment are the bedrock of successful execution. (Bernard Quancard)

Execute Value, Deliver on Customer Relationships and Commitments: Thoughts about a Coach

By: Dennis J Chapman, Founder and CEO
The Chapman Group

After my 60-plus years in life, and 40-plus as a business professional, I am convinced that everything I needed to be successful—the skills, traits, and disciplines—I learned on the fields and courts where I played competitive sports. So it's only fitting that to illustrate the concepts of what it takes for a strategic account manager and his or her team to execute value and deliver on relationships and commitments I will lean on the lessons I learned from the coach who made the largest impact on my life.

A few years back, I had the opportunity to play three years of Division I basketball at the University of Massachusetts for Jack Leaman, who is the winningest coach in school history and a member of the Boston University Athletic Hall of Fame ('77), The UMass Athletic Hall of Fame ('88), and the New England Sports Hall of Fame ('03). In other words, Jack was an incredibly successful person. But Jack was only as prosperous as his teams were—meaning his career was fully dependent on the routine successful execution of plays by a handful of 18-to-22-year-old boys, which, based on what we know about men this age, may not always have been the easiest task. But Jack was able to get 12 rowdy alpha males with grandiose hoop dreams to simmer down and play for one another with a singular team focus and dream year after year after year. It's fair to say that pondering Jack's success and trying to incorporate what I learned from him into my own life was a substantial undertaking early in my business career.

Fortunately for me, Coach and I had forged such a strong relationship in those three years at UMass that, for years after, I could still call him to pick his brain for advice or whatever wisdom he wished to bestow upon me during our conversations. While Jack never really came right out and said, "This is how you win…," I eventually was able to piece together his advice into the following three principles for executing success:

1. Measurements (statistics, metrics, and analytics) are the lifeblood of executing successful decision making.

2. Relationships must be managed because executing success is rarely done on one's own— especially when operating in a team environment.

3. Commitment to executing success must be mutually shared amongst all of the key stakeholders.

I have personally utilized these principles, in different flavors for different processes, throughout the duration of my business career, and they have served me well and helped me realize great success. Naturally, they seem like the first place to start when analyzing what it truly takes to execute value inside of a strategic account. And wouldn't you know it, these same three principles will provide the perfect framework for your organization to successfully execute value inside your strategic accounts. To put it simply:

(Executing) Value = measuring impact + managing relationships + mutual commitment

For the rest of this chapter, let's draw the connection between the role of the strategic account manager and that of Coach Leaman, who was tasked with executing and delivering value (i.e., winning) to his customers (the team) and other stakeholders (the university and fans). Now it is my job to translate how Jack used the equation above to become the winningest coach in UMass history into the principles and methods that will enable you, the strategic account leader, to execute value for your customers.

Measuring impact

Jack, and the entire UMass men's basketball team, had a plethora of measurements, statistics, and analytics at our disposal: points per game, speed, field goal percentage, number of turnovers, height, rebounds, assists, and on and on and on. There was a statistic to measure everything that happened on the court—even in my day. But an inventory of these measurements is far less important than their application. As our leader, it was Jack's job to determine which statistics and metrics to utilize to formulate a game plan for each opponent that would put us in the best position to win. Whatever the strength or weakness of our next opponent, Jack had metrics at his disposal to analyze, crunch, and use to formulate a winning game plan. The decision-making process by which Coach made his game plan was quite simple: accentuate the gains/advantages and minimize the losses/disadvantages. So before we did anything, Coach was able to formulate a winning game plan by maximizing our advantage gaps and minimizing our disadvantage gaps through the use of metrics, measurements, and statistics. This game plan directly influenced and fed our action plan for that week, be it drills in practice, conditioning schedules, the starting five, or what-have-you. But more on that later. For now, let me translate for you the process by which Coach utilized statistics to drive results into principles for executing value.

Similar to my college basketball team, you, as a SAM and business professional, have countless measurements and metrics available to you. The hardest part for you is going to be determining which are the most impactful and valuable to you and, most importantly, to the customer. While your organization may have the quietest HVAC units on the market, it is eminently possible that your customer doesn't value lower sound levels in their HVAC solution—so such a metric is not impactful in their tallying of your organization's value. Therefore, it is critical that you take the time to understand what each specific customer organization values, how they will be measuring these values (i.e., "success"), and what factors impact (positively or negatively) these customer-defined values.

Do not assume that all customers value the same thing or that revenue/profitability are the only metrics that organizations use to determine value. Take the time to discover what the customer organization is looking to accomplish and ask them, "How are you measuring success this year?" Only by gaining a solid understanding of the success metrics the customer organization is using will you then be able to align your own metrics and measurements to speak their language.

Alignment of your organization's measurements and metrics to those of the customer is the only way that the two organizations' numbers will speak the same language and deliver the same impact. They need to be aligned both in scope/magnitude units of measurement. If you want to convince a healthcare provider of your value by talking up new revenues, when the provider is calculating its own successes by patient turnover, then any concept of value will be lost in translation. It is your role as the leader to align your own success metrics into the customer's own metrics for success. Once translated and aligned, then you and your team are ready to begin building the metric-based value proposition. You do this by calculating the total value to the customer by aggregating both positive and negative impacts into a metric-based summary that you can present to the customer for collaboration and validation.

Managing relationships

At some point people have to engage with people. This is as true on the basketball court as it is in the boardroom; as good a tactician as Coach Leaman was, the final outcome was still determined by the execution of plays by a handful of college kids. So what can we learn about the importance of managing relationships in executing value from my old coach? Lots!

Jack had a reputation as "a player's coach." But after playing for him, I quickly realized that he was not "just" a player's coach. He was also a coach's coach, an alumni coach, a faculty's coach, a reporter's coach … You get the idea. Jack was the coach to everyone in and around the university. And while the number of people with whom Jack had ongoing relationships was too expansive to enumerate, it's paramount to understand how much Jack truly valued each of those relationships—no matter how big or how small—because he believed that each of them added value to the UMass basketball team and our shared goal of winning.

This is the first lesson Coach Leaman can teach us about managing relationships when it comes to executing value: Expand your relationship network to include everyone you can. This doesn't mean you have to build trusted advisor status with everyone you meet in and around a customer's organization, but to effectively execute value you will require a wider breadth of relationships than you imagine. Sources of your value can come from anywhere within your organization and its product/solution portfolio; it is YOUR job to uncover how these sources align with your customer. And the best way to discover those linkages is to expand your relationship network. Go high, wide, and deep throughout your customer's organization; executing value requires you to have multiple relationships at all levels and functions at your customer. This expansive network will enable you to uncover what would have been otherwise hidden positive and negative opportunities to align the value of your organization, team, solution, and brand (i.e., your message) to the business drivers of your customer.

The second lesson I learned from Jack about managing relationships is that, while a wide breadth of relationships can help you to spread your message and discover new sources of value, to accomplish the internal selling required to secure buy-in for your value requires having the RIGHT relationships. Let me explain by introducing you to Ray Ellerbrook, who was the captain of our team and the closest thing that Jack had to a coach on the court. Ray played so many roles for Jack—the communicator, the peacemaker, the messenger…whatever Jack, the team, or the university needed Ray to do, he did. Ray was a Jack disciple, and in business terms he served as the champion for his teammates and everyone who surrounded the team as well. To translate Ray's role into your own world, he would be the one who sells the message internally, who helps secure buy-in, who serves as your closest and strongest relationship inside the customer organization. Any success of the relationship between your company and your strategic account will be wholly dependent on that relationship with your champion. Without a proper champion in place at the customer organization, there is absolutely no way to execute value.

As I said before, strong relationships alone won't help you justify your value. Your relationships have to be at levels of your customer where value can be built, understood, and acted upon. As a strategic supplier, you will be wasting everyone's time if you present and try to execute value for people within spheres of influence at the organization who won't "get it." Typically value can only be justified and understood at the higher levels of an organization. And while I believe this to be mostly true, it comes with one caveat: You need to look beyond job title for other indicators of "the right relationships." It is my experience that there are others who will understand, buy into, and help sell properly executed value (beyond your champion) within the power centers of influence within your customer organization. And they won't always have the job titles you expect.

The final lesson I learned from Coach that is pertinent in your quest to better execute value for your customers is that, the farther you can move up the trust chain, the easier this process becomes. Put the hard work and effort in early to build rapport and credibility. Mutually define, agree to, and over-deliver on commitments. Do whatever you can to move the trust needle in a positive direction. Coach Leaman led by example when it came to this. His door was always open, he was an excellent listener, and he communicated clearly his thoughts and expectations. His greatest gift as a coach may have been his ability to create a culture of openness, collaboration, and competitive comfort on and off of the court. We (the team) always knew that he had our back, and literally nothing would get in the way of doing what Coach asked of us. And this was all thanks to the high level of trust between coach and team. No one ever doubted his personal commitment to our team and personal success.

There's no way to sugarcoat it: To execute value, there has be collaboration built on trust, transparency, and mutual agreement on actions. Otherwise, your story of value and commitment won't be properly told, and your ability to effectively deliver the positive business outcomes the customer expects from its investment in you and your organization will be lost. Executing value is a high trust exercise, and it requires a 110 percent commitment on both sides. Which brings us to the final principle I learned from Coach …

Mutual commitment

I can vividly remember the following phrases (in some form) from some of those early conversations I had with Coach as I was deciding where to bring my talents:

"If you commit to the University of Massachusetts, the university will commit to you."

"If you come to UMass, you will have my full commitment."

"Committing to this team will repay you."

Honestly, I cannot say if this approach was intentional, but Coach was consistent in his message about commitment. Even after I'd joined his team, he continued to preach a gospel of cooperative commitment. What stands out to me after all these years is that, to Coach, commitment was never a one-way street. It was always, by definition, mutual. In all of those statements and throughout my conversations with Coach, whenever the concept of commitment surfaced, it was positioned within a mutual win-win framework.

This is an incredibly important insight, and if there is one thing I would want you to take away, it is this: You will never execute, communicate, and validate value, or build the necessary high-trust relationships to do so, with unidirectional commitment. If there is only one party in the relationship that is consistently committed to the relationship, a climate of resentment will build and destroy any possibility of executing or validating value.

So what can you do as a strategic account leader to ensure mutual commitment in the relationship?

If you are starting from "scratch," the first thing to do is to find some worthwhile short-term win-wins. If you are beginning the journey up the trust ladder, you need to build commitment, credibility, and trust. The following best practices for gaining and maintaining mutual commitment require a certain level of trust between supplier and customer.

To succeed as a leader in this endeavor, you will need these three things:

1. Something to drive and measure mutual commitment

2. A way to create and manage (new) mutual commitments

3. A formal venue for reviewing both

The practice that will best drive and measure mutual commitment is a **joint scorecard**. The purpose of the joint scorecard is to serve as a measurement tool where both the strategic customer and strategic supplier assess one another's performance against a set of agreed-to performance drivers/activities that influence the accomplishment of mutually agreed-to strategic priorities, e.g., value creation, higher quality standards, or a more collaborative relationship. The expectation is that performance gaps may be identified that, when addressed, will enable the successful accomplishment of the agreed-to priorities.

The best practice that will enable the development and management of mutual commitments is the **collaborative action plan, or CAP**. The CAP is a co-developed, constantly evolving plan that is revisited during ongoing business reviews and other appropriate meetings between a strategic customer and one of its strategic suppliers. The purpose of the plan is to formalize the mutually agreed-to efforts over a designated timeline, including roles and responsibilities associated with addressing a mutually agreed-to issue, opportunity, initiative, or priority. A CAP can include any or all of these.

Finally, you will need a formalized venue to review these two items with the customer: the external business review. The purpose of this practice is to place all of the primary stakeholders from the two organizations in a room where they can freely, openly, and transparently review the performance of the relationship through the joint scorecard and call out what has to happen in the existing collaborative plan.

■ CASE STUDY

The situation
A recent client was having difficulty getting a strategic customer to appreciate all the value delivered by the supplier. In fact, the supplier felt like it was being pushed into the commodity box. After careful examination of the situation, we discovered three important issues. First, the supplier didn't have a key contact at the customer with the power to change the direction of this tide. Second, in most cases the supplier's extra value efforts ("value-adds") were being executed without recognition and little if any involvement from, or validation by, the customer. And last, the customer hadn't even committed to being a part of these initiatives, leaving the two organizations misaligned in their priorities and commitments.

The remedy
The account team began a strategy of identifying the right champion at the account. After pinning him down, they involved him and a core customer team in the development of initiatives that were aligned to customer priorities and documented these efforts in a collaborative action plan. They then collaborated with the customer on a joint score-card made up of key performance metrics tied to success. And finally, they developed a methodology and associated calculations to monetize the positive financial impact they were delivering through these extra efforts.

The result
Today, despite being in a market that could be termed a commodity business environment, this client brings in greater revenue than ever from a broader portfolio of customers. This is a very simple example of the success that's possible when executing value is supported by managed relationships and mutual commitments by all. ■

Conclusion

It can't be a coincidence that I also have coached basketball (albeit at a far lower level) and had similar success to Coach Leaman. I'm not the all-time-winningest coach at any Division I programs, but I did routinely coach my son's travel team to ridiculous winning records, typically playing more than 50 games a winter up and down the East Coast against quality competition and never once losing more than 10 games in a season. Could it be that I simply had better players to coach? Maybe. But I prefer to think that it was those principles that Coach Leaman instilled in me. For a basketball team to be successful, I've developed this equation to replicate a winning culture on our team:

Winning = (statistics x game planning) + (right coaching x right players) + mutual commitments

As a strategic account manager and (future) business leader, I used the same principles and concepts to construct a similar equation that would provide the key to forming mutually beneficial relationships between customers and suppliers:

(Executing) Value = measuring impacts + managing relationships + mutual commitment

Unfortunately neither Coach Jack Leaman nor Captain Ray Ellerbrook is here with us to appreciate the impact that they had on my life and the lives of so many others. But I do know we can all share in the value they provided. For this and much, much more I thank them for the opportunity to learn, explore, and have a meaningful business and personal life. And to you, the reader: May you also follow these same principles and share in similar successes as well.

Chapter 17

SAM is a journey. The strategic account manager doesn't manage projects or opportunities but rather a strategic corporate relationship. It's not about delivering projects but about having a continuous and long-lasting impact on customer business outcomes. The SAM is the manager and orchestrator of a strategic productivity journey with the customer, not a closer of deals. In this chapter, we will see how critical it is to use the voice of the customer and to establish a dashboard composed of customer metrics to allow for the effective managing of the overall business relationship.

The business cases that Walker covers in this chapter are all good illustrations of managing a customer relationship through time, rather than just managing deals. The common thread between each case is the idea that strategic account management is a customer productivity journey, rather than just the management of deals or projects. The objective of managing a corporate customer relationship is to bring innovative ideas, build trust, enhance reach, and attain trusted advisor status for the SAM, which should be the ultimate objective for all SAMs with their strategic customers. (Bernard Quancard)

Realize and Expand Value through Overall Relationship and Outcome Management

By Patrick Gibbons
Principal, Senior Vice President
Walker

and

Jeff Marr
Vice President, Solutions Development
Walker

In this section we'll focus on realizing and expanding value with customers through effective management of the overall customer relationship and desired outcomes. This zeroes in on step 7 of the SAMA SAM Process, wherein strategic account managers strive to strengthen their relationship with customers to expand share of wallet and achieve the role of a trusted advisor.

Four key elements are at the heart of this step: (1) gaining a deep understanding of the customer's business, (2) being a strong advocate for your customer within your company, (3) developing a solid measurement to monitor progress, and (4) bringing relevant ideas and solutions that show your commitment to customer success. While there are many ways to develop these elements, this section will focus on several key tactics proven to make a difference.

The mid-contract opportunity

Like it or not, most of us tend to do our best work when the situation is urgent—or at least that is when we give something our full attention. In the life of a strategic account, there are several key times when this is very common: when we're competing to win business, when we're getting things up and running, when a problem arises, and when the account is up for renewal. At each of these times, the pressure is on and we're focused on delivering as much value as possible for the customer.

Unfortunately, the opposite is also true. When things are running relatively smoothly—typically, when an account is in the middle of its contract—we tend to turn our attention to more pressing matters. We can easily be lulled into a false sense of security, only to find out later that our customer was never very happy, and at the time of renewal we end up fighting to keep the account. And when we scramble to bring our best work to our client, who could blame them for saying, "You're too late!"

Seizing the opportunity that exists at the mid-contract stage with an account is an effective way to avoid such surprises. The mid-contract stage is the ideal time to evaluate the value you are delivering to your customer and identify ways to deliver even more value.

■ CASE STUDY: Cushman & Wakefield continually evolving its client relationships

Most professional service businesses work hard to sustain client relationships as long as possible to counter the high cost of finding and adding new clients. Global commercial real estate is no exception to this rule, and Cushman & Wakefield (C&W), a $3 billion giant in this space with offices in 60 countries and more than 45,000 employees, has undertaken a unique approach that earns longer-term client relationships and more renewals. They call the approach an "account assessment."

For its largest strategic accounts, C&W conducts an assessment in the middle of the client contract period. This means a client will receive a formal account assessment two to three years into a five-year contract, and this is in addition to business reviews and client meetings it conducts on a quarterly and annual basis. Barbara Desmond, a senior managing partner, summed up the benefits of the more intense assessment: "Our clients deserve hearing about the latest and greatest we can offer them and hearing that sooner than later—certainly sooner than at the rebid presentation." Cushman & Wakefield had sustained double-digit growth and high renewal rates even before the new process began—but just the small risk of lost business with clients this size has made account assessments well worth investing in.

C&W's account assessment program draws from a variety of internal functions and teams, all facilitated in-house. New "players" are invited to rotate into each assessment, including subject-matter experts who are not engaged in day-to-day activities. This cross-functional team collaborates with the account team and various role players supporting the account and also participates in interviews with client contacts. The assessment team identifies the successes, challenges, weaknesses, and opportunities for improving the relationship and increasing value delivered to the client.

The current state of the relationship is explored in depth as well as the best practices that could be incorporated into the relationship. The assessment team then analyzes the findings and delivers recommendations for the account team to confirm and discuss with the customer.

Critical to the process is the action plan with a timeline specifying tangible benefits to the customer—things like enhanced processes, cost savings, risk mitigation, and simpler decision making. Then by executing these changes and improvements, C&W positions itself more strongly for when the client rebids the contract and compares C&W services to its competitors.

As one key to success, Desmond stressed communication and the need to assure the account team and client of the value the process can bring. Clients see the fresh ideas with input from experts and can rest assured that the best-fit services and newest practices are being considered.

Cushman & Wakefield breaks down the total solution and services it provides, with questions posed on subjects like:

- The contract
- Tools offered by C&W that enable facilities management
- Reports offered by C&W

- Metrics used most or needed to do the job
- Working with C&W people
- Working with C&W processes

The client and account teams are asked about what the customer wants most, if they receive all they need now, and whether other improvements or better practices might be available. In addition to probing about the current state, clients are asked how their businesses are changing and what they want in the future or in an ideal state.

For each recommendation, the team documents steps it will take to implement changes, identifies potential obstacles, outlines the timeframe to implement, and estimates the cost in man-hours and dollars. Perhaps the most important purpose of the assessment is to determine the payback to clients and to C&W for each recommendation in terms of cost reductions, efficiencies gained, enhanced decision making, and risk mitigation.

The C&W account team and other resources are aligned around proposed changes, and then the project is executed collaboratively with the client. Updates are given quarterly and annually.

This process has paid dividends for Cushman & Wakefield and its clients, including:

- Increased revenues through high renewal rates going even higher
- New internal relationships and bonds formed
- Better shared learning from and across subject-matter experts in a global organization
- Expansion of services, scaling of innovative approaches
- Celebration of successes

Clients of C&W have attested to the benefits of seeing best practices and services sooner than they would otherwise as well as enjoying better reports and streamlined processes. In general, customer feedback praises the assessment for helping leverage the capability of C&W as a strategic service provider. ■

Use journey mapping to jump-start mid-contract strategies

It's clear Cushman & Wakefield has a proven system in place for leveraging the mid-contract opportunity. But how can you implement this discipline in your organization? One useful approach to getting started is journey mapping. This involves gathering insights from inside your organization as well as from customer contacts. You begin by having the key players on your account team, as well as other key individuals from functional areas across the business, to literally map out all the interactions and steps the customer goes through while working with your company. Typically a facilitated exercise, the group posts dozens of sticky notes along a blank wall to chart the customer's journey and then digs deeper to determine strengths, weaknesses, and key "moments of truth" that can make or break a customer relationship.

A second or parallel step is to have corporate staff or third-party experts interview customer contacts regarding the partnering relationship. The topics explored may include the customer's changing plans, unmet needs, new solutions, additional support, and any other relevant topics. Once all content and inputs are documented, the findings are grouped and analyzed to determine the most essential implications for action-taking. In short, the analysis should take the form of identifying:

- **Strengths.** What moments of truth for the customer do you perform so well as to be leverageable, i.e., part of the reason your customer buys from you versus a competitor or via self-service?

- **Opportunities.** What experiences for the customer, if improved or better monetized, would make enough difference to your customer as to become a leverageable strength?

- **Weaknesses.** What issues for the customer take priority for fixing, i.e., moments of truth where performance falls short and negatively affects the relationship?

Finally, you will create a set of recommendations and planned initiatives based on an analysis of the inputs as well as collaboration with selected customer contacts. The goal is for the customer to agree that your team proactively invested in providing refreshed and improved approaches for the duration of the contract in advance of any RFP that may be issued. Journey mapping is a highly interactive and engaging process that motivates teams to take action. Effectively implemented during the mid-contract stage, it is an excellent way to discover new opportunities to deliver value to your most strategic accounts.

Leveraging the "voice of the customer" for growth

Strategic account managers are pretty good at acting on customer feedback. The data from SAMA's latest "Survey on Current Trends and Practices in Strategic Account Management" backs this up. When asked to rate their skills and abilities, SAMs rated "acting on customer feedback" as their top skill. Impressive! Since it is clear SAMs respond well to requests and input during their normal day-to-day interactions, do they really need anything else?

Actually, a more formal process of gathering feedback through surveys and other techniques serves as an excellent complement to the daily interactions of a SAM. Here's why: A structured voice-of-the-customer program provides feedback that is more comprehensive and objective. It is in this environment that customers are more likely to share the positives and negatives of the relationship. And often, there are surprises.

While SAMs may feel like they know their customer better than anyone else (and probably do), it is impossible to know everything. And sometimes those knowledge gaps result in revenue losses for the supplier. This can be particularly true when trying to understand the perspective of senior-level contacts who may have been involved in original purchasing decisions but now may have less day-to-day contact with the account team.

It's important to have a solid voice-of-the-customer program that collects useful customer insights, provides a solid rating for each account, and prompts action to address issues and leverage opportunities. Such programs are typically administered in a different part of the organization, so it is important to search out the person or department that administers your customer listening program and make sure you're getting the customer insights you need to serve your customers.

■ CASE STUDY: Leveraging the "voice of the customer" at Johnson Controls, Inc.

Johnson Controls, Inc. (JCI), a global company with core businesses in the automotive, building, and energy-storage industries, conducts an extensive customer experience program that leverages the voice of the customer across its company. This highly visible initiative creates a constant flow of customer insights that influences strategic direction and fuels quality improvements, service enhancements, and overall focus on customer issues and concerns. Among its most important benefits is the use of objective customer feedback to monitor and improve the company's most strategic relationships.

Key ingredients of JCI's voice-of-the-customer initiative include:

- Gathering the right insights from the right people through a variety of methods
- Creating awareness to engage customers and employees through visibility and access
- Creating improvement initiatives, with accountability, at all levels based on customer priorities
- Providing links to other information sources to demonstrate a quantified ROI for the business
- Aligning customer feedback to each employee's job and aligning it with corporate strategy
- Creating a network of cross-company customer advocates

These initiatives clearly demonstrate JCI's integration of the voice of the customer into all levels of the organization in a way that is actionable, drives results, and includes the SAMs. "Strategic account managers are likely the most important users of customer insights," said Daniel Viera, JCI's global manager of customer experience. "Because they interact directly with the customer on a regular basis, they can immediately put feedback to use to leverage an opportunity, address a concern, or respond to a request. These are our quickest wins!"

Customer feedback is made available to SAMs in a variety of ways. First, they receive feedback provided by each individual involved in their account. Input from these contacts is seamlessly delivered to them via the customer relationship management (CRM) system they use every day, making it easy for SAMs to view, interpret, and respond quickly to ratings and comments from individual customers.

Customer feedback is also provided at an account level, where input from all the contacts within a strategic account are rolled into one report. This provides the SAM with a concise view of the entire account relationship, revealing key metrics, ratings, and comments. These reports are shared with all strategic account managers, distributed by email, through their CRM system and via SharePoint.

Finally, the customer experience team conducts one-on-one meetings to review customer feedback, provide perspective on the results, share important trends, address any questions, and ensure the SAMs have a complete understanding of the insights provided by their customers and can determine appropriate action steps. The customer experience team also provides a format for action planning which is tracked using customer dashboards within the CRM system. Monthly update calls also ensure that the customer experience team is available for any additional support.

"Our strategic account managers do an excellent job of managing and growing our most important customer relationships," said Viera. "The role of the customer experience team is to support the SAMs' efforts by providing added insight to help them be more effective in their role and help them deliver more value to our customers."

JCI's customer experience program has resulted in driving integrated, continuous improvement processes across all regions and channels based on the voice of the customer and identifying early operational predictors through the value chain that impact overall customer experience and business relationships. The voice of the customer is embedded into day-to-day business processes and establishes metrics to inform decisions as well as align programs to commercial excellence strategic initiatives. The strategic account managers are key to creating successful results by using and acting on customer feedback. ■

Keeping score: Measuring and monitoring progress

SAMs inherently have a good sense for how things are going with their accounts. Most of the time they can tell intuitively if a relationship is headed in the right direction. However, to objectively evaluate progress it is essential to have a practical way of measuring and monitoring it, and so maintaining a clear scorecard for each strategic account just makes sense. A scorecard provides the structure necessary to objectively track the health of an account and which way it is trending. A solid scorecard also will help gain internal cooperation, secure executive buy-in, and identify areas that demand focus.

While the specifics of a scorecard may vary by company, consider the following five areas as a recommended structure for a strategic account scorecard:

- **Financial success**: to determine if targets are being hit and customer goals are being met. Measures can include spend, profitability, and growth. They can also include customer goals, productivity, operating expenses, and incremental revenue.

- **Execution:** to determine if quality standards and delivery schedules are being met. Measures can include on-time projects/delivery, speed to market, product failures, and problem resolution.

- **Customer insight:** to understand customer feedback and perceptions. Measures can include service ratings, satisfaction/loyalty scores, and customer comments or complaints.

- **Competitive position**: to understand how you stack up with your competition. Measures can include number of suppliers, share of wallet, preferred status or no-bid status.

- **Involvement**: to determine the level of engagement from your customers. Measures can include participation in events, forums, or councils, and willingness to provide references.

Using these five areas as a guide, developing an account scorecard provides a solid structure for monitoring progress and securing support throughout the organization.

■ CASE STUDY: Keeping score at EMC

EMC is a $24.5 billion company with approximately 400 sales offices across 86 countries. With its strategy to enable business customers to transform their operations and deliver IT as a service, EMC works to closely engage its customers. Led by its corporate vice president, EMC's Total Customer Experience (TCE) program has the operational responsibility for engaging EMC's customers, partners, and employees to drive quality, innovation, and continuous improvement into its products, services, and business operations.

EMC is driven by key metrics, and work with its strategic accounts is no exception. Not only does EMC collect a wide range of internal and external metrics, but it has an innovative program to focus on distributing the right metrics to the right stakeholders through highly informative online dashboards.

As background, the EMC Total Customer Experience team distributes voice-of-the-customer, voice-of-the-partner, and voice-of-the-field insights to a broad range of functional groups including sales, service, and other supporting functions. The team also uses supporting data analytics to gain deeper insight into customer feedback and drive continuous improvements based on these insights. "We modified and leveraged existing TCE programs to ensure we collected insights along the end-to-end customer journey," said Jenny Beazley, director of global customer advocacy at EMC. "We want to ensure we know how our customers buy, get deployed, receive support, and use our products."

Delivering metrics on strategic account performance in a digestible and actionable manner is a significant challenge. To do this, EMC created end-to-end account dashboards, which made displaying the array of insights about specific customers scalable and viewable for strategic account managers, global account managers, executives, and sales teams. This tool includes the current status of the account with information across categories, including:

- **Financial success.** The dashboard reveals revenue trends captured over a period of years influenced by the 3- to 5-year buying cycle it sees as typical for a company to perform a refresh of its technology. This information proves to be critical as SAM teams move toward conversations with customers about renewals. This interactive dashboard provides the ability to drill down by revenue source for hardware, software, professional services, consulting, and other services and solutions provided by EMC.

- **Execution.** This portion of the dashboard focuses on quality events such as issues the customer has experienced that impact its satisfaction with the product. Often, quality incidents will connect with a corresponding low service transactional satisfaction score, which is also highlighted on the dashboard.

- **Customer insight.** EMC displays information based on how customers compare to each other in terms of customer satisfaction ratings, Net Promoter Scores, and comparative industry ratings. What's more, EMC segments its strategic accounts into four key categories representing its customers' level of loyalty to EMC: "truly loyal," "accessible," "trapped," and "high risk." This breakdown helps account management teams tailor their approach to the customer based on the customer's overall relationship with EMC.

- **Competitive position.** Data in this section comes from industry feedback from a large panel of IT professionals. The information, which is specific for each industry EMC serves, provides a snapshot of the competition and how EMC stacks up. These insights help strategic account teams understand the competitive landscape and deliver important perspective for their day-to-day interactions.

- **Involvement.** The dashboard also provides a perspective of customer involvement and engagement. EMC has found its most engaged customers, for the most part, will respond to its global customer loyalty program survey, from which it derives a Net Promoter Score. The dashboard clearly displays the proportion of those customers that are categorized as "promoters," "passives," or "detractors." ∎

The trusted advisor: Bringing ideas and building trust

What does trust look like in a strategic account relationship? To capture this, consider this somewhat obscure quote from Woody Allen: "Someday the lamb will lay by the lion … but it won't get much sleep."

Strategic account relationships are much the same. No matter how much trust is built or earned, SAMs always need to be proactive and alert to ensure that relationships are constantly growing. Because mergers, reorganizations, and other sweeping changes that are completely out of the SAM's control are so common in today's business environment, constant attention is vital to continually earn and maintain trust.

To develop deep, trusting relationships a SAM must do more than manage day-to-day activities. Rather, he or she must establish a format for having thoughtful discussions where ideas can be shared and trust can be built. A proven technique is to conduct quarterly business reviews (QBRs) with strategic accounts, where stakeholders can remove themselves from their day-to-day duties and focus on the bigger picture.

The concept of QBRs isn't a new or earth-shattering idea to most strategic account managers, but consider two questions: (1) Have you sustained your practice of holding these business meetings with your key account(s) each quarter? And (2) how robust and strategic are the meetings for you and the customer?

Group meetings have prompted awkward, or even humorous, responses when strategic account managers are asked a simple question: "How often in a year do you hold quarterly business reviews with your strategic customers?" Sheepishly, half the group typically admits these meetings don't happen consistently each quarter. Some say they started well but let the cadence of regular meetings slip. Others never established QBRs as a regular practice. However, all tend to agree that the main challenge is making these meetings mutually valuable.

We strongly believe the responsibility for initiating QBRs rests with SAMs and their teams, although planning should include the customer's input. Four key ingredients are necessary for successful QBRs:

- **The right preparation.** To prepare for an effective QBR, strategic account managers should collaborate with their accounts to compose a joint account scorecard. Different from the scorecard mentioned earlier under the subhead "Keeping score: Measuring and monitoring progress" (which is for internal use only), this is a jointly developed listing of shared goals and metrics to be reviewed at the quarterly meetings with the customer (the QBRs).

- **The right people.** For QBRs to be highly effective, the right people must be involved. This includes economic buyers, technical buyers, and usage buyers as well as executives who have a vested interest in the value delivered by your products and services.

- **The right agenda.** The heart of the QBR is the content. These meetings should evaluate business impact, review activity, provide updates on company and industry news, share best practices, and chart the path forward. The tone should be collaborative, ensuring the customer can sense the SAM's commitment to seeing its success.

- **Effective follow-up.** SAMs can strengthen the effectiveness of a QBR by following up on commitments, sharing additional insights, listing action items, and using other methods that demonstrate commitment and follow through.

Quarterly business reviews can be a highly effective way to ensure your organization is not just another vendor. Implemented effectively, they can be an excellent method to becoming recognized as a reliable, trusted advisor.

■ CASE STUDY: QBRs at Viavi

These four key elements for effective QBRs are clearly evident in the quarterly business review program at Viavi Solutions, a provider of software and hardware platforms that deliver end-to-end network test and visibility solutions across physical, virtual, and hybrid networks. Viavi uses these meetings to connect with its customers on a strategic level, making sure customer goals are met, issues are addressed, and new ideas are discussed for future success. QBRs at Viavi require careful advanced planning to assure a successful outcome. Beginning more than a month in advance, the date is set and participants are invited to attend. Viavi typically casts a wide net to encourage broad attendance, all guided by the topics that will be discussed. At least two weeks in advance, Viavi SAMs work with their primary customer contacts to agree on a productive agenda. Based on the topics, they collaborate with the customer to develop a joint set of slides that is sent to all parties one week prior to the meeting. Those who attend are expected to review the material and be prepared for the discussion.

Joint account scorecards are updated and distributed in advance of the meeting as well. In many cases these provide a report card on Viavi's performance based on established target metrics. The agenda for Viavi's quarterly business reviews includes a host of strategic topics that are important to both the company and its customer. These may include:

- Current challenges, concerns, and company happenings that may be of interest to both parties. This could include upcoming mergers, shifts in manufacturing locations, management changes, budget constraints, and other issues that could affect day-to-day work together.
- A review of current accolades from both parties to include top awards, technology breakthroughs, recent big wins, or strong performance. This review encourages support for each other's successes.
- A review of the product roadmap as well as new technology or services being provided by both parties
- Ideas and new services being developed by Viavi to make it easier to do business together
- An in-depth report card review. This includes dialogue on all pertinent metrics that have been established and discussion regarding plans to improve any metrics that fall below targeted scores.
- Discussion of any opportunities for improvement that might fall outside of report card review
- Feature topic discussion, which may include a guest speaker from within the company to expand on an agreed-upon subject to improve the business relationship
- A summary and review of any old or new action items

After the meeting, detailed minutes are prepared that include a running action register, ensuring that all those involved are well informed of any changes or developments.

"Quarterly business reviews are an essential element in developing strong relationships with our most strategic customers," said Darin Stowe, senior customer program manager at Viavi. "There's no question this is the most valuable time we can spend with our customer, collaborating in a way that encourages mutual respect for each other and shared success for both organizations." ■

Chapter 18

SAMA research shows that the most successful SAMs come from organizations with strong, embedded enablement initiatives, by which we mean specialized training, focused coaching, and the use of technology to enable efficient SAM work. The importance of technology in SAM enablement is increasing every day and is the focus of this chapter. With the scope and complexity of the SAM role continuing to grow, technology is the only way to guarantee good SAM work productivity. Additionally, the SAM's effectiveness will come largely from access to concrete business cases and role playing, both of which will be enabled by technology. Last but not least, SAM enablement must include tailored coaching that uses technology to create a formalized framework, allowing coaches to have impact on data, inputs, assumptions, analyses, and actions as formulated by the SAM in the management of his or her customer relationship. This is the most critical way to increase SAM performance and business results, and the chapter ahead provides a tremendous executive summary of how technology can and should enable SAMs to perform in their jobs. (Bernard Quancard)

Enabling SAM through Technology Designed for Strategic Account Management

By Jerry Alderman, CEO
Valkre

Brian Kiep, COO
Valkre

We increasingly live in a digital, connected world that moves fast and changes rapidly. Tried and true approaches to developing new products are being replaced with ones designed to make minimum viable products that are OK to "fail fast." Project management has shifted from following a linear script of tasks and milestones to working in agile teams that can communicate and iterate quickly. Meanwhile, B2B customers are starting to demand real-time solutions similar to what they experience as consumers.

Strategic account management programs have not remained untouched by this new connected, digital world. Demands are being placed on companies to work with customers to create value faster than competitors can. Falling behind on this dimension is akin to giving competitors the upper hand, whereas excelling here provides a unique opportunity to create differentiation and grow faster. The SAM has to adapt and learn how to live in this world.

Adding people and introducing new protocols can hardly help a SAM program become faster, more agile, and more transparent. Rather, the next competitive advantage will come from speeding up your co-value creation engine with the help of technology.

The role of technology

Good technology takes business processes and makes them better. That's why people use it. In the world of SAM, this primarily involves three processes:

1. **Enabling SAMs.** SAMA has codified the work of a SAM into a series of steps that exemplifies an efficient value-creation process. In the digital age more and more SAMs will demand that they have an application to help them do this work rather than relying on manual, disparate tools that are slow, out of date, and not connected to the customer.

2. **Coaching SAMs.** The work of a SAM is not simple. The primary role of SAMA is to help SAM programs get better. In a faster world, getting better means more real-time coaching. Doing this effectively and at scale requires data, access, and transparency.

3. **Integrating SAMs.** A key role for the SAM is to personalize the value a company can provide for its most critical customers, which requires collaboration and coordination with many different functions internally, such as marketing, product management, and engineering. Shepherding these resources and influencing them without authority can be a time-consuming exercise without tools to create accountability to execute and streamline collaboration.

Enabling SAMs

SAMA has defined the work of a SAM as the driver of the co-value creation process for a company's most strategic accounts. This work is highly specialized, so it's unreasonable to expect it to be system-enabled by an out-of-the-box CRM system. CRM systems can be instrumental in a company's commercial operations, as they typically serve as the source of truth for many value-capture processes such as qualifying leads, managing the pipeline, placing orders, or resolving customer issues. But these systems are not designed for working in a customer-facing way to co-create value.

With that in mind, the options to system-enable SAMs are similar to any specialized undertaking: invest in custom-developed functionality on top of a CRM system or license turnkey software that fits with your organizational needs. The purpose of this chapter is to provide examples of how technology can speed up the work of the SAM and how each step of the co-value creation process can be streamlined and fortified through the use of the right technology.

1. Customer co-discovery & value fit

The co-value creation process begins with the customer's challenges and with you determining your role in solving those challenges. This is typically done in the form of a conversation with key stakeholders. While there are many proven methods of facilitating these discussions, the key to moving fast is having a standardized, structured approach *that results in data*.

Structure and standardization ensure that discovery is being done properly with the customer. This can also reduce the time it takes to execute discovery and the learning curve required to do it well. Data makes it easier to share the customer's perspective internally and with the customer. This is especially important when there are many key stakeholders within a customer whose various perspectives likely differ from one another and can oftentimes conflict. When you can offer actual data, it becomes easier to highlight for the customer similarities and differences within the account in order to better align on where to focus the co-value creation effort.

Enabling SAMs in this area should involve providing "one click" preparation for discovery sessions and extremely fast, mobile capability to document those discussions. Results across conversations should be easy to aggregate and segment, the information should be readily available from any CRM account profile, and this should all serve as the basis for the co-value creation effort.

■ CASE STUDY

A SAM program was struggling to discover new growth opportunities that would yield sustainable, competitive differentiation from its competitors. These efforts had always been managed through customer value scorecards that SAMs filled out manually, meaning they spent more time on issue resolution than on customer co-discovery.

In an effort to fill the funnel more efficiently, the company rolled out a standardized annual discovery effort, enabling the SAM to document his company's past co-value creation efforts and catalog future challenges. This tool helped the SAMs generate discussion guides, gave them a place to document their notes, and produced documents that made it easy to follow up with key stakeholders.

Formalizing this effort with the help of technology yielded double the growth opportunities for strategic customers, mostly in the form of new projects and proposals. Because this effort streamlined what had previously been a manual, *ad hoc*, and time consuming process, this pipeline growth didn't add to the SAMs' workload. ■

2. The strategic account business value plan

It is essential to formalize the SAM process into a strategic account business value plan, and, while this element has been covered in the first part of this book, we want to remind the reader here that technology is essential to making the strategic account business value plan both a relevant (and real-time updated) information system AND a management tool for co-creating value with the various internal and external stakeholders. Again, the strategic account business value plan will ensure internal alignment to customer value opportunities and should help optimize the execution of value and measure the value delivered through customer metrics included in the plan. Technology is an unparalleled way to update in real time the co-created value as well as value expansion opportunities.

■ CASE STUDY

A global automation firm offers a perfect example of how a complex business value plan can only be managed through the smart deployment of technology. This company manages thousands of products, in hundreds of different countries, with thousands of key stakeholders in the end-user ecosystems, including machine tool builders, installers, engineering, and many more. This volume of touch points and data points could only be managed through the use of a fully automated business value plan. Without it, the company would be stuck with a simple repository of information that couldn't be strategically managed to align with the complex organization around its global customers. ■

3. Co-create value

With an effective, data-driven approach to identifying co-value creation opportunities, the next step of SAM enablement is making it easier to co-create win-win solutions. Co-creation is a process that requires a clear understanding of the expected value to be delivered to the customer, visibility on how you might be rewarded for the effort, and the effort required to deliver. Achieving this typically requires the collaboration of many individuals, internally and at the customer, with the SAM playing the central leadership role.

The key to speeding up co-creation is coordination. SAMs should have a living, breathing list of co-value creation opportunities that represent incremental ways to make customers better off. These value targets should include a personalized value proposition that demonstrates how that specific customer can benefit, and this value proposition should be visible to internal and customer experts and should be backed up with action plans and a monetization plan. Being able to quickly document and communicate the process of co-creation helps align the team around the co-value creation effort.

Another way to speed up co-creation is to not have to continuously recreate the wheel. SAMs should have the ability to "copy and tweak" value propositions that have been proven to work.

■ CASE STUDY

A financial services provider was struggling to rejuvenate its relationship with a strategic account plagued by a lack of executive engagement and, hence, a lack of urgency to move on a significant new opportunity. While the SAM and his team had spent the requisite time understanding the customer's challenges and how his firm could ameliorate them, the team lacked the "punch" the SAM felt he needed to spur executives to action.

To highlight the business impact of their solutions, the SAM and his team developed a digital portfolio of co-value creation targets that included a series of value propositions that, in total, represented several million dollars in projected revenue. Thanks to a value quantification tool developed by the company's marketing department—and using real customer inputs, supplied by the customer, to arrive at its value propositions—the SAM was able to standardize how he quantified each value proposition, yielding a suite of proposals that constituted a plan to co-create value. Compare this with the company's legacy process, which would have involved a 75-page PowerPoint presentation using flimsy or hypothetical data to arrive at its conclusions. This collection of value propositions, which was only possible thanks to the company's use of a SAM-enablement tool, resulted in immediate engagement by the C-Suite and the launch of a co-creation process that guaranteed near-term renewal and growth of the program. ■

4. Mobilize and align the multifunctional team

The SAM needs to be a skilled leader and must be able to influence without authority. How that is operationalized will vary from company to company (and even team by team), depending on variables like team size, reporting structure, and geographic location. The role of technology in this step is simple: It should provide broad visibility and accountability.

Imagine an account team member who is supporting multiple value-creation efforts across a variety of accounts. This could even be a "second job" for this team member on top of existing functional responsibilities. If the SAM is doing his or her planning and execution in a way that's disconnected from the team, he or she is not being efficient. SAMs should demand the ability to "cloudify" their co-value creation plans in a way that creates a center of gravity for the team by formalizing plans and streamlining the sharing of information. Instead of emails, Excel, PowerPoint, and SharePoint, think about social collaboration, mobile, reports, and integration.

■ CASE STUDY

A U.S.-based company was trying to increase engagement with a strategic account in Brazil ahead of a purchase agreement renewal. Through its discovery efforts, the company learned that its customer felt disconnected from the supplier due to a lack of local resources to support its growth efforts. Relocating resources wasn't feasible due to the supplier's need for centralized global support by its engineering and product management functions, and hiring local resources to support its efforts would be cost prohibitive.

The company addressed the problem by deploying a customer-facing portal to give both the customer and the supplier's U.S.-based support resources a real-time view into the company's ongoing co-value creation efforts. The portal allowed the company to share news, feedback, and files while reducing its dependency on meetings and emails. The turnaround time to ideate and execute dropped dramatically, and the customer decided to assign a senior procurement resource as the "owner" of the portal to help streamline value delivery on their end. The end result was the renewal of a commercial agreement that had been in serious jeopardy. ■

5. Capture value through negotiation and closing

The way a SAM captures value for his company as a result of his co-value creation efforts can vary dramatically depending on business models and sales processes. Regardless of how a SAM captures value, the key to reaping the reward for that created value is being crystal clear about his or her differentiated value proposition.

For those SAMs who grow accounts deal by deal, technology can help by providing a link between their value proposition development efforts and their sales process. After all, every sales process states that there must be a strong value proposition, and the strongest ones are those that have been co-created and vetted with customers ahead of the deal. Practically speaking, this means making sure that the SAM's customer-facing value proposition development work is connected to the SAM's sales process.

For those who operate in more of a "flow" environment, in which the SAM is working to influence purchase decisions across many transactions, technology can help with negotiations by tracking co-value creation efforts over time. Keeping the thread intact from "Where is what the customer said?" to "This is what we did about it" and "Here are the results" is critical, but it can be complex to hold together. Having a system that connects these dots for a SAM and the customer can help capture value when it comes time to negotiate and close.

■ CASE STUDY

A company's strategic account was in the midst of significant turnover among key decision makers right ahead of issuing a critical RFP. On top of this, the supplier company's main competitor had recently been acquired, putting it in position to deliver a much stronger offering than in the past.

In advance of the negotiation process, the SAM diligently documented past co-value creation efforts and built a new value proposition that promised significant operating cost savings. Since the new value proposition was based on data that had been organized and validated by the customer, all the SAM had to do was summarize this information in his proposal and attach the co-value creation details as support. The result was a 60 percent increase in expected revenue from the deal and the preservation of a price premium that had been imperiled. ■

6. Execute value and deliver to customer commitments and orders

This step is the least intrinsically strategic step of the SAMA value-creation process, but it's probably one on which SAMs spend too much of their time. In its simplest form, this stage is about SAMs having an agile, co-value creation scorecard that creates clarity on what is being done to deliver value. This should not be a task list. This should be a scorecard that logs all the initiatives that will directly impact the customer's business.

This work doesn't feel strategic because it is about "doing what you said you were going to do." However, the use of manual, disparate methods to keep the information up to date leads to a lot of wasted time. The tools SAMs need to enable their execution on value are relatively straightforward. They need a simple, fast program that houses status updates, latest news, meetings minutes, and other pertinent items, and which doesn't require spending time formatting presentations or pulling information from across variable portals. The information on these scorecards should be widely available to, and easily decipherable by, all internal and external stakeholders and should form the basis of a regular operating rhythm. With less time spent preparing for meetings and making sure all account team members are aligned, the SAM will be free to spend much more time on more strategic work.

■ CASE STUDY

A company's siloed structure was making timely execution an ongoing struggle. Keeping key stakeholders in the loop was made difficult by the company's reliance on manual processes and the use of files hosted in disparate locations. To rectify the situation the SAM program leadership established digital scorecards for more than 20 strategic accounts covering more than 300 co-value creation projects. The company developed digital status reports, which it published to the organization by region and P&L and which it integrated into its CRM system. In less than a year, the SAM program improved its rate of on-time delivery from 50 percent to more than 90 percent. ■

7. Realize and expand value through overall relationship and outcome management

With the results of the co-value creation process digitalized and wired together from beginning to end, the SAM has all the information she needs to manage the relationship and outcomes of the co-value creation process. This starts with putting in place a co-value creation scorecard that is aligned with the customer's key metrics. This scorecard should be backed up by a real-time accounting of specific initiatives that are directly contributing to the customer's business outcomes.

The key to making this successful is thinking of the scorecard as an "agile" tool that drives the conversations at each major review. A living, breathing scorecard shows what's been delivered recently, what's next, and what is open to change. The process of co-value creation ebbs and flows with customer challenges and doesn't correlate with your account planning cycle. The more your measurements can match the speed of your customer, the more powerful the scorecard can be. Finally, as this scorecard and supporting details should be the basis of any strategic relationship, this information should be broadly available internally and to customers.

■ CASE STUDY

One company's strategic account requested a thorough tally of the total annual cost savings generated by the supplier's co-value creation initiatives. Managing and validating this information can become an insurmountable administrative burden when the numbers on the scorecard are open for debate. Rather than increasing the resources it allocated for measuring and reporting, the company developed a cost-savings scorecard that automatically updated at the completion of every initiative. Just as critically, the scorecard required multiple customer stakeholders to personally validate the supplier's value-creation efforts and associated cost savings, ensuring the cost savings wouldn't be disputed at the end of the year. The scorecard was designed to function as a dynamic, real-time dashboard displaying cost-savings data, which would support further co-discovery of value opportunities. ■

Coaching SAMs

By enabling the SAM with technology, the result of his or her work becomes data, rather than files. This does wonders when it comes to optimizing a company's ability to coach its SAMs for the purposes of skill development and improved work output. By simply providing access to the SAM's work, coaches can help improve their effectiveness in three ways:

- **Real-time visibility.** With data comes access. Most technologies today are cloud-based, meaning the work done by a SAM is instantly available to coaches. This not only saves time and reduces the effort to collaborate, but it can fundamentally change how a company decides to upskill its SAMs. Instead of spending hours in the classroom and hoping concepts "stick," training time can be minimized and skills developed in real time as the work is done.

- **Standardization.** Inherent in any organization is variability in the way work is done. While specifying how every action should be undertaken is probably not the answer for everyone, installing "guardrails" can be an effective way to move faster and with more agility. For example, when a new SAM takes over an account, being able to coach from an existing dataset on that account can be tremendously important during the transition.

- **Quality.** SAMs are put in place for customers that generate critical revenues, profits, and growth opportunities. They are also humans whose skills and talents vary. Coaching then becomes a critical part of ensuring that all work is completed up to the company's standards. Technology and data make this much easier.

The key theme here is data. If the work product of a SAM is data, then it becomes much easier to provide cost-effective coaching by leveraging cloud-based technologies.

Integrating SAMs

While SAMs are a critical part of any commercial operation, they don't work in a vacuum. There are many moving parts, from product management and marketing to field sales and executive management. Many times the SAM has no direct authority over these functions and spends more time fighting internal battles than focusing on co-value creation. Here are three ways technology can help support SAMs to free them up to drive growth:

- **Integration.** Even though CRM is not designed to manage customer value, it is often the source of record for a company's commercial operations. If a company takes advantage of turnkey applications designed for co-value creation, SAMs may find it easier and faster to "bring their own interface." This could mean making it easy to access the growth strategy from an account profile in CRM or developing rigorous value propositions for a particular opportunity. Any customer value application worth its salt will make it easy to integrate the work of a SAM into the rest of a company's commercial operations.

- **Value intelligence library.** In most cases SAMs do not invent a company's offerings. Their special skill is in personalizing their company's offerings for their strategic accounts' specific business needs. The key here is the word *personalize*. It is difficult to personalize anything without a general understanding of its value, and in most companies the only resource available is an out-of-date product catalog that focuses on features or technical specifications instead of customer value. Creating a "source of truth" for value propositions in a way that SAMs can quickly access, copy, and personalize for a customer co-creation opportunity can save time and improve quality.

- **Enterprise reports.** Despite the importance of a strategic account, sometimes it is difficult to get an organization to operate account by account. For example, a product manager in charge of helping to deliver pilot projects has to work across customers to be effective. By the same token, investment in a new technology might require the voice of several strategic customers to push through internal decision making. Reports that can aggregate data across many strategic accounts and are packaged to a specific role can go a long way to creating the accountability required to execute on behalf of customers.

Getting started

With cloud technology it is easier than ever to get started using technology to take a SAM program to the next level. Gone are the days of having to go through huge enterprise software implementations. Instead it can be as simple as following these three steps:

- **Start Small.** Pick three to five accounts, a technology provider, and get to work. Build momentum by demonstrating quick wins. Improve the system and make it as simple as possible. Natural demand for expansion will occur as more in the organization can "feel" the benefits of technology. If at all possible avoid the CRM ecosystem at first; it can be very slow, since these systems and processes are not designed for the work of a SAM. Continue to add accounts at a pace that makes sense until you reach a critical mass.

- **Integrate.** Once you achieve critical mass, it is time to make the technology stick. This typically happens by formally integrating the tech-enabled SAM processes with your existing commercial processes. This usually means getting the CRM team involved. Integration helps in a few ways. First, it has a way of legitimizing SAM work as different from what would be done with non-SAM accounts. Second, a new data set is brought to the organization that can help with other core processes, such as innovation and quality.

- **Scale & sustain.** With the infrastructure of SAM technology in place, organizations are in a great position to expand rapidly. This is when Learning & Development can craft programs to upskill SAMs quickly and put coaching in place to support expansion. This is when the outcomes can formally be made part of job descriptions and performance reviews and when continuous improvement can happen quickly based on changing needs, markets, and competitors.

It's important to remember that the key is to just get started. Competitors and customers are not waiting for you, but there's still time for companies to get ahead and stay ahead. Those programs that commit to becoming faster, more agile, and more transparent are going to be the ones that win the most with their customers.

Part 3

The Role of a SAM

By Elisabeth Cornell
Chief Knowledge Officer
SAMA

The role of a strategic account manager exists to fulfill the business objectives of a corporate-level, customer-centric strategy designed to ensure the firm's future for long-term growth and profitability. Hence, the requirements of the SAM job and the desired knowledge, competencies, skills, and attributes of individual SAMs must align directly with those objectives.

To understand what is needed and required in a SAM, it is essential to understand this alignment of purpose to a C-level, rather than sales, strategy.

In brief, the SAM role has evolved over the past several decades to meet the increasing demands and organizational complexity of critically important and usually very large clients, many of whom grew over time from large territorial accounts to national accounts and then to international and global accounts. Customers' commercial interests and internal capabilities expanded over time, driving the installation of new systems to centralize purchasing, enable enterprise coordination, and consolidate their supplier bases for efficiencies and global consistency.

Within supplier firms it became a business management necessity to manage these particular clients differently in order to viably assemble and integrate the firm's offerings, realign internal management and operations to deliver to a higher set of expectations, and compete to provide a more sustainable customer-supplier relationship.

At the same time, by virtue of becoming more customer-oriented—by first focusing on the needs and aspirations of the customer, rather than its own agenda—a supplier could shift into a more proactive mode of interaction tied to the circumstances and priorities of its customer, with the prospect of uncovering even greater opportunities to generate the supplier's own goals for growth. It was a strategy to grow with the customer on a continual basis rather than by single project engagements.

This shift, however, required a different mindset than the predominant salesforce view of buyers as adversaries. After a point, even the strong personal and social relationships nurtured by a single salesperson who considered herself the "owner" of the account could not alone satisfy the customer's larger business demands and respond to the pressures of commoditization. A salesperson selling just product fell (and still falls) mercy to negotiations based largely on price.

What the advanced or mature customer wanted transcended product features and benefits; the customer wanted and needed the supplier to demonstrate an improvement or value to the business—to the bottom line. Not only that, but mature customers needed their suppliers to solve business problems and address strategic objectives with solutions that could be delivered however, whenever, and wherever the customer wanted them.

However, most firms are structured in silos for internal efficiency and coherence, as opposed to being organized around customers—what SAMA's president and CEO, Bernard Quancard, calls "the third axis" (the first two being product and geography). Consider the experience of one of your strategic, key, or global clients being called upon by four or more different salespeople from different divisions representing different products and/or geographies, without benefit of a cohesive value proposition, coordinated services or delivery, and without regard to the impact on the client's time, business operations, and efficiencies. What about the missed opportunities for an integrated solution optimizing both price and overall value for the benefit of both the client and the supplier?

The emerging role of the SAM grew along with the organizational need to manage the entire business of a strategic customer centrally, from a perspective of understanding the customer as a whole instead of just its parts—its organizational structure, strategy, and priorities—and from which an entire account strategy could be formulated, based largely on (1) the size and scope of potential profitable business with that customer and (2) the supplier's ability to utilize its best assets and capabilities to sustainably win, deliver, and realize value for the company and customer.

From this central position, a single strategic or global account manager could create a cohesive customer value proposition, identify and mobilize the key internal resources and stakeholders, and centrally orchestrate customer interactions, aiming for a seamless customer experience across the company's different business units and geographies.

Rather than manage the account as a "lone wolf," the manager of a strategic account would create "a village" to build a strategic customer relationship at an enterprise level—to develop a core internal team as well as an extended network of relevant experts and functional talent across the company and among its own suppliers. In effect, the customer became a corporate account of the company and an organizational priority of the entire enterprise.

The business outcomes of successfully executed strategic account management offer significant benefits to both supplier and customer based in large measure on a mutual acknowledgement of their synergies and collaborative potential to:

- maximize revenue
- minimize costs
- increase productivity
- reduce risk
- develop innovative solutions
- drive continuous improvements

The customer's view of the supplier, the maturity of its buying organization, and its willingness to act collaboratively and constructively with the supplier also are critical aspects of a strategic relationship and, in fact, are hugely relevant in the initial determination and designation of an account as "strategic." This is discussed in detail elsewhere in this book. However, it is the earned mutual regard and willingness to collaborate that becomes the springboard to lift the SAM up to a higher level of customer engagement and a greatly expanded pipeline of opportunities.

The role of management

Here it is important to comment on the role of a supplier's C-level and senior management who, in charging a SAM with enterprise responsibility and accountability for a strategic customer relationship, must:

- take an active role in empowering the SAM to work across the company
- raise awareness and understanding of the importance of strategic accounts to the firm
- help facilitate organizational alignment between silos and across country borders and continents
- create top-to-top relationships with each of the firm's most strategic customers

"High-performance SAM programs sensitize top management to required role changes, obtain management support to resolve rigidities and frictions, and clarify how the roles of people involved in SAM will change in terms of their tasks, responsibilities, and competencies," says Axel Thoma, research partner at the Institute for International Management, in Switzerland. "A transparent explanation of SAM roles helps reduce ambiguity and unfounded fears. Groups that perceive an imminent threat to their decision-making power, such as country and business line/unit managers, may engage in hidden turf battles, but putting all the cards on the table presses SAM opponents to engage in an open dialogue, which may weaken their counter-productivity in the face of management."

A SAM will perform most effectively with an elevated status inside his or her own organization to support his or her efforts to influence and collaborate with colleagues who, most commonly, are not direct reports. In many leading firms with mature strategic account organizations, senior SAMs function at a vice president level or equivalent to a country general manager, and top-level GAMs often function in a post-VP position.

Having worked daily over decades with these organizations that strive to embed the role of a SAM in their companies, SAMA has found executive support to be a major point of conflict and frustration, for SAMs and senior management alike. Regardless of a SAM's individual talent, personal attributes, and persistence, the absence of C-level and executive support for the SAM's status and, indeed, the whole strategic accounts initiative has been seen to disenfranchise SAM endeavors and make alignment to the customer virtually impossible. Data collected from SAMs over the years reflect this effect regarding their major internal obstacles, as exemplified in Figure 22 from SAMA's "2014 Report on Current Trends & Practices in Strategic Account Management."

There are no halfway measures in strategic, key, or global account management; management must be willing to create new roles, new infrastructure, new HR policies, and new processes to succeed. I recall speaking with one company executive who shied away from the idea of making any major changes to his current organization because he didn't want to "rock the boat." Well, establishing an entirely new role and position of a SAM, formalizing it with corporate HR, and legitimizing it to the salesforce and to the rest of the company will rock the boat. Otherwise, a SAM will never get on the boat! It's critical that the SAM be an accepted and well-regarded member of the organization. Figure 23 shows how the global logistics company DHL formalized its entire account management organization.

Figure 22   Top internal barriers facing strategic account managers

SAMs indicate greatest internal barriers in retaining/developing strategic relationships

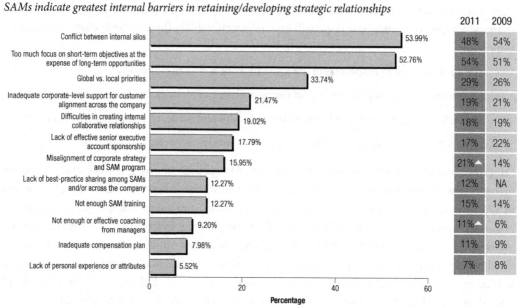

△ / ▽ Indicates a statistically significant increase/decrease over previous year ratings at a 90% confidence level.

Figure 23   Account management at DHL

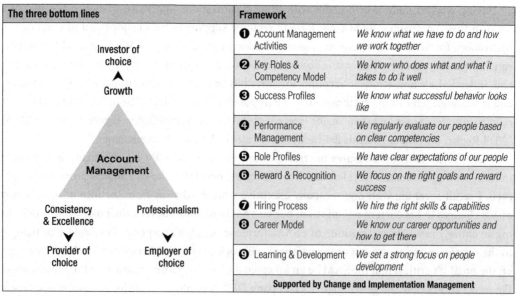

Source: DHL

Empowering SAMs and elevating their status lends authority to their role and its importance to the corporate strategy. Creating a distinct brand for the SAM within the company and with customers also helps to attract and retain top talent, which is integral to the elevated status of a strategic account within the company. Consequently, the customer receives the benefits of access to this talent due to its designation as a strategic account.

Core requirements of a SAM

Given the context in which the role of a SAM evolved and became established, and the implications of the type of talent and leadership needed to fulfill the oversized expectations for the job, let's turn now to the core requirements of the individual best suited for this position—the desired competencies, skills, and attributes—that are linked most closely to the primary business objective of creating mutual customer-supplier value through a series of key activities represented in a SAM process.

Part 2 of this book, which focuses on the SAMA SAM process, details an interdependent set of steps that, when formalized and undertaken with discipline, serves as a roadmap for developing and sustaining a successful strategic customer relationship, coordinated mobilization and alignment of internal resources, and effective execution of a business account plan, resulting in the realization of documented business outcomes. While in reality the process isn't linear, a collaborative progression to the realization of mutual value is the goal.

In SAMA's view, a major distinction of the SAM's role and process is the extent of connection to, and collaboration with, the customer. In each step of the SAM process there is a need for, and expectation of, customer engagement. The SAM process is above all a collaborative process, internally and externally, and the success of the SAM depends largely upon his or her ability to actively involve and enlist the right stakeholders for the right reasons at the right times.

On several levels, this is a departure from conventional selling methodologies that insist on the seller's "control of the relationship" and "control of the conversation" with the customer. This attitude can be at odds with collaboration and tends to promote or reinforce what the customer may perceive as adversarial behavior, and it may diminish the moments of opportunity to learn something new from the customer. If the customer is already behaving in an adversarial way, trying to exert control may only waste a chance to change the tone and direction of the conversation. It's very difficult to actively listen to your customer and build greater customer intimacy and trust if you're expending all your energy on trying to control every aspect of the interaction. Focusing on the quality of interactions is more consistent with the role and objectives of a SAM.

In addition, the scope of the SAM's job clearly goes far beyond other sales positions, including in these important aspects:

- The status and significance of the customer's business to the company's financial health

- The extent of risk and accountability that the SAM assumes for both internal and customer KPIs

- The degree to which the SAM must frequently work across a complex internal matrix to influence and galvanize others to create and deliver an integrated solution of products and services to the client

- The higher level of executive customer engagement required to sell value-based solutions and foster collaborative innovations

To summarize, a short definition of a SAM could be worded as follows:

The job of a strategic account manager is to develop and sustain a long-term strategic customer relationship for mutual growth, profitability, trust, loyalty, innovation, and risk management. The strategic account manager must leverage the company's enterprise resources and capabilities to create and deliver value-based solutions. These solutions must meet the customer's and company's requirements and expectations as well as create future business. The strategic account manager is at the center of the account team and must be a dynamic leader who can work at all levels and, pivotally, serve as the central point of contact for internal and external executives and stake-holders, to drive results and document value.

SAM competency model

In alignment with the corporate strategy, defined SAM role and job, a SAM competency model is needed to help identify and develop the individuals best suited for the position. A useful and effective competency model can be both simple and comprehensive at the same time—simple enough to be easily understood and workable for HR, managers, and SAMs, and comprehensive enough that it covers all major areas of individual ability that are core to the SAM's job and successful performance.

The model pictured in Figure 24 is the culmination of decades of research of evolving SAM practices in SAMA member companies and across all business sectors including basic materials, consumer goods, financial services, healthcare, industrial goods, technology, and utilities. Benchmarking mature, highly-developed strategic account organizations was especially helpful in pinpointing the skills and competencies these companies identified as essential to the SAM role within their firms. We coupled this data with insights gained from our daily interactions and work over the last several years with SAM program leaders, executive management, managers of SAMs, and SAMs of all types and levels of experience, as well as with our expert network of external consultants and academics.

Figure 24   SAMA Best-in-Class SAM Competency Model®

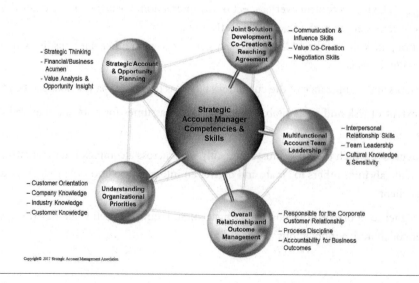

While there exist some important differences in the implementation of strategic account management within various industries' business models, there is remarkable consistency around the foundational skills desired in strategic account managers. Similarly, the challenges of identifying and developing these skills in the right people are widely shared. (Two industries where these core skills and competencies have been modified are healthcare and government. In both sectors, certain government and/or professional regulations prohibit or eliminate certain selling/engagement behaviors as specified in the SAM process.) Just as the implementation of strategic, key, or global account management varies by firm, business model or industry, the role of the SAM must be adjusted also.

The SAMA Best-in-Class SAM Competency Model® identifies five areas of job competence or capability as well as the three or four primary skills associated most strongly with each one. Under each competency is a short numbered list of the key behaviors, actions, and/or activities most relevant to that skill. It is expected that all skills overlap naturally into different competency areas, but for the sake of clarity and manageability of a working model, the skills paired with a single competence are considered of paramount importance to that particular capability.

SAMA's SAM competencies and skills defined

Competency 1.0 – Understanding organizational priorities

Ability to understand your company's and the customer's industries, markets, and business models … Determines customer's buying behavior and metrics for supplier relationships … Maps organizational structure and relationships to identify champions, influencers, and decision makers … Understands your company's corporate strategy and business objectives, and those of the customer … Documents knowledge of everywhere the customer "touches" your company and everywhere your company could potentially touch your customer … Profiles the customer's competitive position vis-à-vis its competitors as well as your competitors' positions vis-à-vis the customer … Identifies the key internal company stakeholders and functional resources currently and potentially required for effective management of the customer's business and opportunities.

Skills
- Customer orientation
- Company knowledge
- Industry knowledge
- Customer knowledge

Competency 2.0 – Strategic account & opportunity planning

Ability to incorporate business intelligence and determine a go-to-market strategy through internal planning sessions … Defines and manages the solution development process, develops a differentiated value proposition, and values the ROI for both the customer and the company … Manages funnel of short- and mid-term opportunities and pre-formulates specific project management requirements … Provides for post-deployment customer support and evaluation … Requires the ability to engage the customer in the planning process.

Skills
- Strategic thinking
- Financial/business acumen
- Value analysis and opportunity insight

Competency 3.0 – Joint solution development, co-creation & reaching agreement

Ability to communicate credibly and effectively at the customer CxO level, demonstrating understanding of the customer's financials and financial strategy ... Provides thought leadership on the customer's business issues and priorities, uncovers and validates key challenges ... Engages the customer in the account planning process and works collaboratively to identify value-based solutions ... Co-creates innovative solutions in areas of highest joint potential and innovation ... Quantifies the differentiated solution/value proposition *vis-à-vis* competitors demonstrating mutual ROI ... Sells high and wide throughout the customer organization, managing Procurement and multilevel relationships with the support and coordination of the account team ... Negotiates and reaches agreement on company engagement and specific deals, specifying resource commitment and allocations internally and at the customer.

Skills • Communication & influence skills
    • Value co-creation
    • Negotiation skills

Competency 4.0 – Multifunctional account team leadership

Ability to create a team vision and strategy for effective account plan development and execution ... Builds and aligns the account team to the customer's key functions and requirements, jointly developing team goals and KPIs ... Establishes trust, motivates and coaches team members through regular communications ... Inputs information on account data, activities, and best practices ... Structures role and deployment of internal executive sponsor/s for account team goals and customer relationship objectives.

Skills • Interpersonal relationship skills
    • Team leadership
    • Cultural knowledge and sensitivity

Competency 5.0 – Overall relationship & outcome management

Requires accountability for the sustained health and improvement of the overall customer relationship through regular business reviews against the performance dashboard and customer communications ... Maintains and augments role as a trusted thought leader in individual customer relationships and owns the customer satisfaction/loyalty metrics ... Maintains the internal network of relationships and aligns the internal and external commitments leading to execution of company and customer requirements and the achievement of desired business outcomes.

Skills • Responsible for the corporate customer relationship
    • Process discipline
    • Accountability for business outcomes

SAM competency assessments and current performance

The use of a SAM competency assessment tool is highly recommended for evaluating your SAMs' current abilities and should be aligned to whatever SAM competency model your firm uses. SAMA has developed a 360 degree-type tool that assesses the proficiency of a strategic account manager (or equivalent position) for the competencies and skills detailed in the SAM competency model described herein.

The assessment, which is completed by the SAM, manager(s), optional peers, directors, and/or customers, establishes a baseline of maturity of skills and competencies and focuses the dialogue between SAM and manager on the right areas.

The competency assessment integrates the role of the SAM's manager, who sits down with the SAM to discuss the report in an open and honest dialogue. The two can acknowledge and celebrate the areas where there have been successes and excellent outcomes, recognize strengths and weaknesses, and formulate a plan for improvement including time for coaching, additional training, and re-evaluation at designated intervals to document and discuss progress.

As of October 2016, more than a thousand SAMs from more than a hundred companies (along with their managers and peers) have completed a SAMA competency assessment. A considerable portion of these individuals were newly enrolled in SAMA's Certified Strategic Account Manager (CSAM) program, with many recently promoted to a SAM position, primarily from their general sales organization. A smaller portion had prior SAM experience. The assessment provides a benchmark from which to measure progress at a future interval following the completion of their SAM curriculum, coaching, and application of their skills to their strategic account work.

Figure 25   SAM competency pre-assessment – skills summary

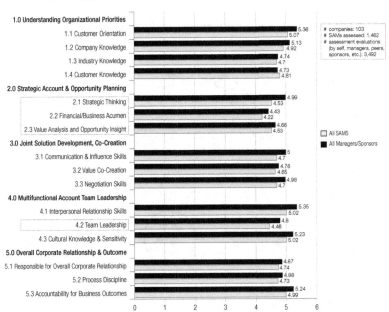

The aggregate of these SAM assessment scores is interesting to examine and reveals those critical competencies and skills that appear to be least developed in SAMs overall, according to their managers. These areas of greatest need are framed in Figure 25. These are good examples of the signature skills that, while essential to performing the SAM's job, have not been previously required or strongly developed. Quite often we find gaps between how SAMs rate themselves and how their managers rate them, which represents a perfect launching pad for a discussion around potential areas of improvement.

The global SAM/global account manager (GAM)

SAMA believes that the foundational competencies and skills of a SAM are the same for a global SAM. However, the size, complexity, and practical challenges of a global account, versus a national or multinational one, enlarge the degree of risk and responsibility, indicating a need for not only a highly experienced SAM but also a number of proven talents in specific areas, including:

- Engaging customer C-level executives
- Fluency in global practices and global citizenship
- General business and P&L management
- International team leadership
- Record of performance
- Being multilingual

For these reasons, GAMs in mature strategic/global account organizations are often drawn from a different pool of candidates: the ranks of senior and executive management. This raises important questions about what is the best career path for a GAM versus a SAM. See possible career path options in the Schneider Electric example in Figure 26.

Figure 26 Career horizon for global account managers at Schneider Electric

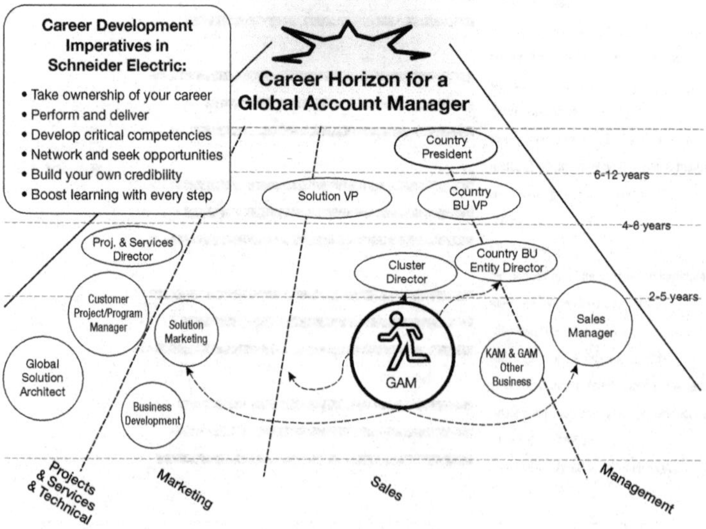

Source: Schneider

Personality and personal attributes

An individual's personality and traits may be the most important consideration in the profiling and selection of the right talent to perform the SAM role, simply because the most desirable personal traits, qualities, and characteristics greatly inform the SAM's behavior and are considered very difficult to develop or teach. While specific competencies and skills as previously described are critical to the job, most of those can be learned and developed through practice and experience, whereas qualities such as honesty, integrity, self-confidence, and self-motivation are mostly ingrained.

Senior executives and sales management recognize the value of certain personality traits in a high-performing strategic account manager whose relationship-building abilities enable success in key activities of the SAM process, such as team leadership, collaboration, influence without authority, reaching agreement, and resolving conflict. The most sought-after traits in a SAM, drawn from SAMA's work with member companies and studies with expert consultants (most notably LaVon Koerner at Revenue Storm) and academics, closely relate to the key behaviors and activities of the SAM job. We believe that they account for some of the differences in results that are achieved by a "great" versus an "average" SAM.

Top 10 personal traits of a SAM

1. Strategic thinker

Both an attribute and a skill, strategic thinking is essential in account planning and many other SAM activities in order to connect the dots between knowledge of the customer and knowledge of one's own company. Strategic thinking may be the most important asset to a SAM, though one of the least understood. While some believe it cannot be taught, a leading authority on the cognitive aspects of strategic thinking and its application to business practices, Dr. Julia Sloan, contends it can be learned and developed, and explains this and much more in her excellent book *Learning to Think Strategically*.

2. Active listener

Several years ago, I attended a firm's in-house training session for 50 or more top salespeople and observed a role-playing exercise in which each salesperson sat face-to-face with a manager who was playing the role of a customer, for the purpose of gathering information. As all 50 began conversing with their counterparts in individual conversations, I merely watched the group's body language. In a short amount of time, I saw that many "customers" were sitting back in their chairs with their arms crossed, silent. The salespeople were leaning forward, talking earnestly, and gesturing to make their points. It was very clear that these conversations were one-sided and that the salespeople were not asking their customer any questions—let alone the right kinds of questions.

Active listening does not come naturally to many people, and the absence of it will rob SAMs of their best opportunities to understand their customer and uncover new information about the person and his/her company. Most importantly, it will cripple their chances of having a meaningful dialogue, building rapport, and potentially collaborating on important issues or new developments. It's difficult to be a strategic thinker if one is not continually acquiring new information and insights.

Obviously, active listening is critical in all aspects of the SAM's job, including working with all kinds of professionals at all levels within the SAM's own firm. There is much more to be gained if a SAM focuses on "being interest*ed* rather than interest*ing*," as the saying goes.

3. Customer focused

Being customer focused is similar to active listening in that it requires a change in mindset—from an internally focused view of self or company to a broader view of others' experiences and priorities. Customer-focused suppliers place a high priority on the customer experience and the customer journey. A customer-focused SAM accumulates deep knowledge of her account to gain constructive and creative insights into potential solutions that will solve their business issues or advance their goals. And a customer-focused SAM is the best person to effectively communicate and represent the interests and needs of the customer inside her own company.

4. Accomplishment driven

Being accomplishment driven has both self- and team-directed aspects. Findings from the SAMA/ Value Innoruption Advisors' 2015 study, "Individual SAM Characteristics Influencing Customer-Supplier Value Realization," found "achievement driven" to be a top trait among SAMs and related SAM professionals who have a high drive to improve their own performance and initiate actions to do so.

The same trait contributes to the SAM's ability to ensure process discipline by mobilizing a multi-functional team, completing a collaborative account plan, and driving execution to customer metrics. Being goal driven is integral to effective SAM leadership.

5. Accountable

The SAM is in a unique position to be able to accept responsibility for decisions, actions, and outcomes impacting both her own firm and her customer's. The SAM is ultimately accountable for the continued health and growth of one or more customer-supplier relationships, the realization of value on both sides, and her personal performance throughout.

6. Creative/innovative

Similar to strategic thinkers, creative people are comfortable with ambiguity and challenging assumptions, and they're able to view a problem or challenge from multiple perspectives. The ability to be creative is at the core of the co-value creation process, where a SAM has an opportunity to differentiate both herself and her firm in a collaborative engagement with a colleague or customer, and can uncover new information, define an unknown need, and generate ideas leading to a novel improvement or innovative solution.

7. Team oriented

Being team oriented is 180 degrees from being a "lone wolf." A team-oriented SAM recognizes and respects the experience and expertise of colleagues for collaboration, cooperation, and coordination of strategic account work throughout the value-creation process. It is well documented by many experts that trust is essential for successful teamwork, and a SAM who appreciates the individual role and contributions of each team member can harness the group's talents for dramatic results.

8. Flexible/adaptable

There are many circumstances in a SAM's life where flexibility and adaptability are not only helpful but absolutely necessary. Given the extensive internal and external organizations and networks of people with whom a SAM interacts, and the frequency of operational issues, interruptions, and obstacles, being flexible is a valuable asset for the SAM's calm under pressure.

9. Organized

Being well organized is a great quality in almost every line of work. However, a SAM must be extremely organized in her own work as well as in every aspect that involves the key players and stakeholders who matter to the strategic account. Much of the work is delegated to others to implement in their functional or geographic capacities, but the SAM must have the master plan and the roadmap to the destination.

10. Analytical

Being analytical is a great tool for a SAM throughout the value-creation process, synthesizing incoming information, analyzing financials, assessing current and potential scenarios of engagements, developing solutions, negotiation, and more. Having the ability to analyze and interpret data, generate new insights, and make calculated judgments and confident decisions all figure into successful SAM performance.

Many more traits also are associated with SAMs, as mentioned in open-ended responses by SAMs and managers of SAMs, in SAMA's "2014 Current Trends & Practices in Strategic Account Management." The personal qualities and attributes that contribute most to success as a SAM, according to the report, consist of the following:

Articulate	Endurance	Socially perceptive
Authentic/genuine	Entrepreneurial	Tenacious
Collaborative	Ethical	Trustworthy
Credible	Resilience	Versatile
Curious	Self-confident	Visionary
Diplomatic	Self-disciplined	
Empathetic	Self-motivated	

Emotional Intelligence (EI)

It's a revealing exercise to reorganize the entire list of personal attributes above according to types as shown here (the top ten are shown in bold), and note that the majority of the qualities fall under Social/Emotional and Self-Management.

Core Values	Social/Emotional	Self-Management	Intellect/Mental Acuity
Ethical	**Customer focused**	**Accountable**	**Strategic thinker**
Honesty	**Team oriented**	**Active listener**	**Creative/innovative**
Integrity	Inspiring	**Accomplishment-driven**	**Analytical**
Trustworthy	Persuasive	**Flexible/adaptable**	Articulate
	Socially perceptive	**Organized**	Curious
	Authentic/genuine	Self-motivated	Forward-thinking
	Collaborative	Endurance	
	Credible	Proactive	
	Diplomatic	Resilient	
	Empathetic	Self-confident	

From a practical perspective, it's easy for management and the SAMs themselves to overestimate the importance of the hard skills while underestimating the value of emotional intelligence. In his book *The EQ Edge,* Steven J. Stein writes, "Emotional and social skills establish…how we perceive and express ourselves, cope with challenges, use emotional information in an effective and meaningful way, and develop and maintain social relationships."[17] According to experts, EI is a predictor of success, as these numbers illustrate:

- More than 80 percent of competencies that differentiate top performers from others are related to EI.
- 75 percent of derailed careers are related to lack of emotional competencies.
- 30 percent of occupational performance is based on EI.
- 67 percent of leadership performance is based on EI.
- 90 percent of high performers are also high in EI.[18]

Leadership

The quality of leadership needed in a world-class SAM is now perhaps more apparent after considering the sum total of the role and requirements, both the hard and soft skills, and the C-level aspects of the position. More than one senior executive has observed that the SAM or GAM is the only person other than the CEO who must work across the whole company. Yet the SAM/GAM has the responsibility but rarely the authority in spanning the business units and geographic boundaries of his own and his customer's organization. This makes the quality of the SAM's leadership more nuanced, complex and unique.

With the growth of globalization in the late 1990s, a new leadership quality was defined in relation to the role of a GAM, which over time has only increased in relevance: the quality of political entrepreneurship.

The authors of "The Global Account Management Study," a research report published by SAMA, had this to say about political entrepreneurship:

"They [GAMs] must be adept at treading the corridors of power. They must know the people to speak to, the buttons to press, and the strings to pull, both in their own organization and that of the customer. They must have developed high levels of trust among the people they work with. All these may be seen as political characteristics.

"They are essentially concerned with identifying and exploiting opportunity, with solving problems that add value to the relationship, and with innovation in its broadest sense. All these may be seen as entrepreneurial characteristics."[19]

This may help to explain what it means to be a true leader in the context of a SAM in a global enterprise. Here, the most highly prized leadership is effected through the skills and personal strengths of the individual, rather than the authority of the position itself.

---

17 Steven J. Stein, Ph.D. and Howard E. Book, M.D. *The EQ Edge*, Jossey-Bass, 2011, p. 13

18 Bo Golovan, Strategic Solutions Associates; Jessica Worny Janicki, JWJ Consulting, LLC; and, Bernard Souche, Medtronic of Canada, Emotional Intelligence for SAM Success. SAMA Annual Conference, 2016. Statistics sourced from *www.eiconsortium.org*. The Bar-On Model of Emotional-Social Intelligence (ESI), Bar-On, R. (2006)

19 Kevin Wilson, Simon Croom, Tony Millman, Dan Weilbaker. "The Global Account Management Study" Research Report. Strategic Account Management Association and The Sales Research Trust, Ltd., 2000, p16. *http://classic.strategicaccounts.org/dlpdf/SAMA-VIA_Report_Value_Realization.pdf*

The future role of the SAM

The SAM role has continued to evolve and adapt along with global economic conditions, changes in corporate strategy and business models, further consolidation of the supplier base, more sophisticated sourcing/procurement practices, e-commerce, the growth of supplier relationship management (SRM) programs, market volatility, and the disruptions brought about by the digitalization of business and the speed with which new technologies and applications are introduced.

The future is being felt now, and the role of the SAM is being impacted and transformed in these critical areas:

1. Supplier end-to-end value management capabilities

In the 2015 SAMA research report "Individual SAM Characteristics Influencing Customer-Supplier Value Realization," the authors had this to say:

> "The core of the SAM's job—to create value with customers—has grown to become an entire value management system that closely weaves together all of the upstream and downstream processes, from co-discovery with customers to solution development, from value quantification/ monetization, value-pricing, and negotiation to value capture and realized sustainable value.

> More than ever, the SAM is charged to provide continuity of the value purpose, preservation of the value proposition throughout, and assurance of the agreed value outcomes. Heretofore, firms have focused and excelled in particular tasks along the value continuum (such as value creation), while neglecting others (value quantification, value-pricing, and value capture). All are now expected in a truly competitive value management capability and greatly benefit firm performance. Newer tools and methodologies now facilitate these specific processes more efficiently."[20]

2. Functional integration

Marketing is an area where new digital technologies have enabled greater connectivity (between humans, humans and machines, and between machines) to customers, through tracking and monitoring of individual customer behavior and activities on the web, as well as creating opportunities to personalize messaging and real-time interactions. Writing in the 2016 SAMA report "The Digitalization Drive," co-author Kaj Storbacka of the University of Auckland proposes that "Account-based marketing (ABM) focuses sales and marketing efforts on understanding the challenges of each contact inside a strategic account, with the aim to design account-specific action plans, to orchestrate coordinated, outbound communication programs, and to measure achieved coverage and levels of engagement inside each account."[21]

SAMA has seen impressive case examples where marketing and SAM teams are now successfully collaborating on account strategy for designated strategic customers, creating new, more efficient processes and data reporting, and becoming a more responsive, agile competitor. SAMs who build their digital acumen will have new leadership opportunities to capitalize on the potential of these

---

20 Value Innoruption Advisors and SAMA. "Individual SAM Characteristics Influencing Customer-Supplier Value Realization" Report. Strategic Account Management Association and Value Innoruption Advisors. 2015. *http://classic. strategicaccounts.org/dlpdf/SAMA-VIA_Report_Value_Realization.pdf*

21 Kaj Storbacka and SAMA, "The Digitalization Drive." Strategic Account Management Association and Kaj Storbacka. 2016, p56. *http://classic.strategicaccounts.org/dlpdf/SAMA_DIGITALIZATION_DRIVE.pdf*

new digital tools and to advocate for organizational changes that will advance their firm's competitiveness in these areas.

3. Customer connectivity and expanding customer-supplier ecosystems

Customers no longer need to turn to their suppliers first for information; in fact, they use multiple media and platforms to acquire knowledge from experts, other customers, and colleagues long before they may want to have a conversation with a supplier. Moreover, increased connectivity enabled by digital technologies is allowing customers to expand their networks in pursuit of making their products and services more innovative and less costly. The result is a larger ecosystem of assorted stakeholders, and the SAM and SAM team need to be similarly connected within this community.

"For individual strategic account managers, it is a question of a shift in mindset," says Storbacka. "They need to think of themselves less as account managers and more as community facilitators. By being present on social media and other platforms they can regularly connect to customers and get educated on new opportunities for value creation."

Moreover, he says, "The role and responsibility of a SAM is being transformed from 'advanced, consultative, insight-based selling focusing on one customer relationship' toward the 'orchestration of mutual value creation in a larger ecosystem of organizations.'"[22]

4. Institutionalizing co-innovation

Innovation within a B2B context can be seen to occur incrementally, often in evolutionary fashion, as well as disruptively precipitating an abrupt change within a short period of time. Customer-driven innovation, or co-innovation, refers to innovation created as a result of direct customer-supplier collaboration. Co-innovation is most likely to occur within strategic relationships where there is already a significant partnership, a willingness to pursue mutual interests, and a strategic fit of objectives and capabilities.

The most successful and frequent co-innovation is now being seen within companies that not only encourage and support such activities but that have ingrained a drive for innovation in their firm's core values and cultural DNA. This level of commitment is generally expressed in their corporate strategy and championed at the C-level. As described by Matthias Heutger, senior vice president for strategy, marketing & innovation at DHL, it is "a systematic enterprise methodology to foster innovation for strategic accounts," taking the form of specific innovation initiatives and programs that deploy company-wide assets and expertise.

"A relentless focus on the future—on trending technology and potential applications to their industry and their customers' businesses—positions the company as a thought leader on innovation. The SAM can invite his or her strategic customer to engage at a high level in the supplier's enterprise activities and organically move them toward specific areas of interest and development.

"In our experience, once DHL and a key account have successfully implemented something new—whether it's a new process, method, solution, or service—and observed its positive impact, both parties typically commit to achieving the next co-innovation, igniting an innovation-based relationship that can continue indefinitely."[23]

---

22 Kaj Storbacka and SAMA, "The Digitalization Drive." Strategic Account Management Association and Kaj Storbacka. 2016, p9. *http://classic.strategicaccounts.org/dlpdf/SAMA_DIGITALIZATION_DRIVE.pdf*

23 Matthias Heutger. "Transforming strategic accounts through systematic co-innovation." *Velocity*, Vol. 17, Issue 3. 2015. *http://classic.strategicaccounts.org/dlpdf/velfall15_feature%203.pdf*

Part 4

The Future of SAM: Five Predictions

By Francis Gouillart
President
Experience Co-Creation Partnership (ECCP)

1. The scope of problems addressed by SAMs will increase dramatically.

Today, SAMs address mostly operational problems with their customers, with a particular emphasis on reducing their customers' costs. A few of them help their customers develop new products or be more innovative. In the future, SAMs will offer their products and solutions in the larger context of global problems in health care, energy, food, or the environment. This will require a breadth of ambition and a vision of the future which comparatively few SAMs have today. The transformational nature of these challenges will demand that SAMs develop a charismatic, nearly spiritual, side combined with an ability to lay out an economically realistic step-by-step path to that vision of the future.

- *Implications for the SAM process.* Five years out, SAMs will spend much more time in the front-end discovery part of the SAM process figuring out what the broad problems are, how their customers can contribute to the resolution of these problems, and how they, as a supplier, can help their customers.

- *Implications for SAM competency.* SAMs will have to become broad strategic thinkers able to conceptualize complex problems and define a connection between their company offerings and the resolution of those problems. This will require that SAMs personally role-model the commitment of their company to the resolution of these problems.

- *Implications for the organization.* Some SAMs will continue to come from sales, but more and more of them will come from other functions, such as R&D, strategy, operations, and other disciplines. As the size of global accounts grows larger to address large societal problems, we will see more and more "two-in-a-box" SAM teams where the visionary component and the project management component are represented by two people joined at the hip in a CEO-COO model.

2. SAMs will become ecosystem captains.

Today, SAMs are predominantly focused on their customer, and in some cases on their customer's customer. In the future, the chain of stakeholders the SAM is charged with building relationships with will extend in all directions.

On the downstream side, SAMs will have to reach into the customer's customer's customer and beyond. Many businesses that were traditional B2B businesses are becoming B2B2C, or even B2B2B2C. This is the case, for example, with the advent of the cloud and software-as-a-service, making the SAM accountable not only for selling to the corporate customer but also for fostering use of the product or service at the individual user level.

On the upstream side, SAMs will be increasingly asked to organize networks of innovative suppliers. As most customers are forcing a consolidation of suppliers, they often cut themselves off from smaller innovative suppliers. To avoid this negative development, customers will increasingly demand that their large ("Tier 1") suppliers orchestrate on their behalf the flow of innovation from these smaller "Tier 2" and "Tier 3" suppliers.

There will also be more and more "lateral" partners involved in the resolution of large problems, forcing the SAM to engage with non-traditional players such as NGOs, public entities, regulators, as well as small data-driven service providers. There again, the SAM will be the natural orchestrator for this complex ecosystem.

- *Implications for the SAM process*: Five years out, SAMs will dedicate a lot of time upfront to the construction of the required ecosystem of players and the putting in place of the necessary data platforms to make it effective. Once the proper infrastructure has been put in place, they will be forced into a world of longer lead time for deals, with higher potential size of projects and greater repeatability of revenues. Because the pressure for short-term results will still be there, they will have to assemble a mix of projects that span the continuum of short-, mid- and long-term, with short-term projects "financing" the riskier long-term projects.

- *Implications for SAM competency*. In their role as ecosystem captains, SAMs will need to be patient and spend time aligning agendas among players with different histories and cultures in order to define a worthwhile project that benefits their firm, while allowing a chain of wins for all participants. This will require the political savviness of an arms negotiator. They will, however, still have to deliver short-term sales as well.

- *Implications for the organization*. Because the assembly of an ecosystem inevitably produces cultural challenges, SAMs will have to educate their own firms on the need for new types of relationships with ecosystem partners and the more co-creative imperative of modern business. This will typically require that functions such as R&D, IT, and legal open up to this new world of ecosystem collaboration, with the SAM acting as coach.

3. SAMs will become large community organizers.

Not only will SAMs have to reach out to a larger number of organizational entities beyond the immediate customer, but they also will have to address a larger population of individuals within each entity, thereby producing an exponential growth of the number of people with whom they need to communicate. Beyond the traditional procurement, supply-chain or shared-service individuals, SAMs must increasingly touch R&D, operations, IT, marketing, sales, and environmental people, as well as C-level executives. This will demand that they orchestrate functional communities across multiple players, for example, to enable accountability of the whole ecosystem for the company's products from a supply chain transparency or sustainability point of view.

- *Implications for the SAM process*. The multiplication of the number of "customers" will demand that SAMs pay more and more attention to understanding roles and responsibilities of individuals in the ecosystem. More than ever, careful mapping of the external community of buyers will be key, as will the mobilization of the internal company resource network against external customers. Most importantly, SAMs will have to watch and understand how these internal and external individuals interact with each other and insert themselves into this flow of interactions.

- *Implications for SAM competency.* SAMs will have to continue to be excellent communicators but will have to rely more and more on "social B2B" tools to reach the necessary constituencies. These social B2B tools today are mostly of a qualitative nature (e.g., idea generation), which is of limited value, but their content will become more and more quantifiable (e.g., tabulation of value), giving users more reason to participate in them. We will see more and more thematic communities of interest form as subsets of ecosystems, and SAMs will have to become curators of these sub-communities, using the increasingly sophisticated IT tools at their disposal.

- *Implications for the organization.* The development of large cross-functional communities of people will force everybody in the future organization to be outward-facing. Nearly everybody will have an external customer, in addition to having many internal customers. IT and Legal will be particularly challenged by the need for SAMs to organize cross-company communities, since their traditional mandate is to fight intrusions inside the perimeter of the company's systems and IT.

4. SAMs will become data bridge-builders.

Products will increasingly become data platforms linking suppliers and customers—or if the platforms are not embedded right in the product, they will accompany the products in some fashion. More and more, the value created by a supplier's product will lie in its ability to improve operations at the customer by providing some form of data that enables the customer to make better decisions. Not only will the data platforms enable better customer decisions, but they will enable an accounting by the supplier of the value created for the customer. The role of the SAM will be to sell not only products but the data platform and services that connect supplier and customer, making the relationship "stickier" and increasing switching costs for the customer.

- *Implications for the SAM process.* The conceptualization of value and the quantification of that value will become more and more indispensable components of the SAM process. Five years out, buyers will likely demand that any purchase be justified by some form of business case, itself rooted in data provided by a real-time system. The Internet of Things will be ubiquitous. This will demand that SAM teams reinforce their ranks with IT development people, analytical people, and data scientists able to compute such value.

- *Implications for SAM competency.* While SAMs will not do any of this analytical work themselves, they will have to become quite proficient at conceptualizing value and providing guidance to the analytical and IT teams on how the data platform setup will enable the development of valuable sales projects. SAMs will need to become "analytical storytellers" able to extract colorful and representative stories from the data.

- *Implications for the organization.* Increasingly, companies will develop small analytical teams inside their SAM organization to support the work of the SAM. These teams will be charged with "blitzing" projects at their front end, mobilizing the necessary communities on the supplier and customer side, creating a first conceptualization of value, and setting up the long-term data platforms that will accompany the project delivery. Some of the analytical people inside those teams will become SAMs themselves over time, after acquiring the necessary relationship skills. As already mentioned, IT and Legal will be challenged by the very concept of cross-company data feeds.

5. SAMs will become value innovators.

Innovation will increasingly occur at the point of contact between supplier and customer, not in the lab. Innovative solutions will be born from the initiative of a few creative SAMs willing to experiment at the edge of established relationships and business models. Innovation will happen when a SAM and his or her customer counterpart start bending the existing model beyond recognition, creating a "first-of-a-kind" blueprint that can then be replicated by others. This will require that SAMs take on the innovation challenge as an integral part of their mission, in addition to the more traditional sales challenge.

- *Implications for the SAM process.* Innovation today is generally a marginal part of most SAMs' roles. It is usually thought of as part of the account-expansion process, once a solid relationship has been established. For example, some SAMs try to include an innovation component as part of the quarterly business review with customers. In the future, the role of innovation will be much more central to and start from the beginning of the relationship-building process. Only SAMs able to commit technical resources to the development of projects will be given access to the necessary decision makers, which will require that the SAMs themselves develop a strong ability to contribute to the innovation agenda.

- *Implications for SAM competency.* SAMs have traditionally deferred to R&D and technical resources on matters of innovation. This will no longer be acceptable, and SAMs will have to demonstrate innovation proficiency to succeed. They will not have to develop the technical knowledge themselves but will need to demonstrate that they can engage with innovation people inside their company and at the customer.

- *Implications for the organization.* Because technical resources are typically not sales-oriented, there is often a large chasm between sales and R&D. Culturally, this is a gap that needs to be filled in two directions. SAMs will become better at innovation, and technical people will become more externally focused. This will require that organizations develop a new process that allows salespeople and engineers to collaborate for the benefit of customers. This will make the SAM program more than "just" strategic; it will become essential to innovation, value creation, and growth. Market share will be won and lost based on who has assembled the best team, internally *and* externally. This entire constellation of stakeholders, led by the SAM, will drive the creation, implementation, and execution of value—leading to new business models, processes, and productivity improvements. The SAM program will no longer be simply an overlay to deal with large, complex global companies. It will become the engine of growth in revenues, profits, innovations, new business models, process improvements, and market reach.

If you're a SAM, welcome to a brave new world!

CPSIA information can be obtained
at www.ICGtesting.com
Printed in the USA
LVOW04*0625021117

554734LV00021B/252/P